Routledge Revivals

THE BLUE REVIEW

THE
BLUE REVIEW
Literature Drama Art Music

EDITED BY
JOHN MIDDLETON MURRY

Numbers One to Three
MAY 1913 - JULY 1913
NOW REPRINTED IN ONE VOLUME

First published in 1913 by Frank Cass and Company Limited

This edition first published in 2018 by Routledge
2 Park Square, Milton Park, Abingdon, Oxon, OX14 4RN
and by Routledge
52 Vanderbilt Avenue, New York, NY 10017, USA

Routledge is an imprint of the Taylor & Francis Group, an informa business

A Library of Congress record exists under ISBN:

ISBN 13: 978-0-367-18009-6 (hbk)
ISBN 13: 978-0-367-18010-2 (pbk)
ISBN 13: 978-0-429-05908-7 (ebk)

ENGLISH LITTLE MAGAZINES No. 6

EDITED BY B. C. BLOOMFIELD

THE BLUE REVIEW

THE
BLUE REVIEW

Literature Drama Art Music

EDITED BY

JOHN MIDDLETON MURRY

Numbers One to Three

MAY 1913 — JULY 1913

NOW REPRINTED IN ONE VOLUME

FRANK CASS AND COMPANY LIMITED
67 GREAT RUSSELL STREET
LONDON WC1

This edition is published by
FRANK CASS AND COMPANY LIMITED
67 Great Russell Street, London WC1
by arrangement

First Published	1913
New Impression	1968

SBN 7146 2103 X

Printed in Great Britain by
Stephen Austin and Sons Ltd., Hertford.

Volume I Number I MAY 1913 One Shilling Net

THE BLUE REVIEW

LITERATURE DRAMA ART MUSIC

Some Contributors to this Number:

MAX BEERBOHM
GILBERT CANNAN
W. H. DAVIES
WALTER DE LA MARE
W. L. GEORGE
W. W. GIBSON
D. H. LAWRENCE
KATHERINE MANSFIELD
FRANK SWINNERTON
HUGH WALPOLE
NORMAN WILKINSON

MARTIN SECKER PUBLISHER
NUMBER FIVE JOHN STREET ADELPHI

MAY

CONTENTS

		Page
A Study in Dubiety	By Max Beerbohm	*Frontispiece*
The Song of the Mad Prince	By Walter de la Mare	1
The Vixen	By Wilfrid Wilson Gibson	3
To His Friend to try Another Tavern	By Oliver Gogarty	4
The Soiled Rose	By D. H. Lawrence	6
The Beggar's Hunt	By W. H. Davies	24
The Esperanto of Art	By W. L. George	28
Epilogue : Pension Seguin	By Katherine Mansfield	37
The Theatre	By Gilbert Cannan	43
Fiction	By Hugh Walpole	46

MAY CONTENTS (*cont.*)

		Page
General Literature	By Frank Swinnerton	51
French Books	By J. Middleton Murry	56
Georgian Music	By W. Denis Browne	63
The Galleries	By Michael T. H. Sadler	68
Review of Reviews: English, French, Italian		71

Drawings by Ambrose McEvoy, Derwent Lees, Harold Squire, and Norman Wilkinson

Editor: John Middleton Murry

Associate Editor: Katherine Mansfield

Editorial Office: 57 Chancery Lane

Telephone 2132 Holborn

A Study in Dubiety — Max Beerbohm

Mr. Edward Marsh wondering whether he dare ask his Chief's leave to include in his anthology of "Georgian Poetry" Mr. George Wyndham's famous and lovely poem: "We want eight and we won't wait."

THE SONG OF THE MAD PRINCE

Who said, " Peacock Pie " ;
  The old King to the sparrow :
Who said, " Crops are ripe " ;
  Rust to the harrow :
Who said, " Where dreams she now ?
Where rests she now her head,
Bathed in eve's loveliness ? "—
    That's what I said.

Who said, " Ay, mum's the word " ;
  Sexton to willow :
Who said, " Green dusk for dreams,
  Moss for a pillow " :
Who said, " All Time's delight
Hath she for narrow bed ;
Life's troubled bubble broken " :—
    That's what I said.

WALTER DE LA MARE

THE VIXEN

The vixen made for Deadman's Flow,
Where not a mare but mine could go ;
And three hounds only splashed across
The quaking hags of mile-wide moss ;
Only three of the deadbeat pack
Scrambled out by Lone Maid's Slack,
Bolter, Tough, and Ne'er-die-Nell :
But as they broke across the fell
The tongue they gave was good to hear,
Lively music, clean and clear,
Such as only light-coats make,
Hot-trod through the girth-deep brake.

The vixen, draggled and nigh-spent,
Twisted through the rimy bent
Towards the Christhope Crags. I thought
Every earth, stopt . . . winded . . . caught . . .
She's a mask and brush ! When white
A squall of snow swept all from sight ;
And, hoodman-blind, Lightfoot and I,
Battled with the roaring sky.

When due South the snow had swept
Light broke, as the vixen crept
Slinking up the stony brae.
On a jutting scar she lay,
Panting, lathered, while she eyed
The hounds that took the stiff brae-side
With yelping music, mad to kill.

Then vixen, hounds and craggy hill
Were smothered in a blinding swirl :
And when it passed, there stood a girl
Where the vixen late had lain,

The Vixen

Smiling down, as I drew rein,
Baffled, and the hounds, deadbeat,
Fawning at the young girl's feet,
Whimpered, cowed, where her red hair,
Streaming to her ankles bare,
Turned as white among the heather
As the vixen's brush's feather.

Flinching on my flinching mare,
I watched her, gaping and astare,
As she smiled with red lips wide,
White fangs, curving, either side
Of her lolling tongue . . . My thrapple
   Felt fear's fang : I strove, agrapple,
Reeling . . . and again blind snow
Closed like night.
                    No man may know
How Lightfoot won through Deadman's Flow.
And naught I knew till, in the glow
Of home's wide door, my wife's kind face
Smiled welcome. And for me the chase,
The last chase, ended. Though the pack
Through the blizzard struggled back,
Gone were Bolter, Tough and Nell,
Where, the vixen's self can tell !
Long we sought them, high and low,
By Christhope Crag and Deadman's Flow,
By slack and syke and hag : and found
Never bone nor hair of hound.

WILFRID WILSON GIBSON

TO HIS FRIEND TO TRY ANOTHER TAVERN

They tell me my friend no transient fit
Has held and holds you where
The muddled mirth and hogshead wit
Pervade the smoke-filled air ;
But that you sit amid largesse
Insisting on punctiliousness.

Pandemian joys should be confined
To those whose bodies lack the mind
That darkens through your eyes.
The time for strenuous things is ripe !
Leave Davus to his greasy tripe
And consequent supplies,
Till Euphuistic calls of " Time "
Cut short the lingering pantomime.

Goodbye to the loose thought that blunts
The insight, and corrodes the soul.
Goodbye to the too frequent bowl :
A long goodbye to Delahunt's.

I know a pub beneath a hill :
  Nine barmaids keep its bar select ;
And keep your corner dusted still.
  Its chucker-out demands respect :
Of those he chucks out everyone
Is locked up by Oblivion.

You've travelled further, friend, than I,
  You're to the Muses better known.
Go confidently in and try
  If they'll serve both or you alone.
I'll talk to him who peeps outside. He
  Will tell me if I'm bona-fide.

To his Friend to Try Another Tavern

The Past is ours : but—what's far more—
  The Future can be catered for,
It's Spirit's in the Still.
  Give it some rare etherial taste
  So men may, when we're gone to waste,
Exclaim : He mixed it well !

OLIVER GOGARTY

THE SOILED ROSE By D. H. LAWRENCE

IT was a mile nearer through the wood. Mechanically, Syson turned up by the forge and lifted the field-gate. The blacksmith and his mate stood still, watching this self-assured trespasser. But Syson, dressed in stylish tweeds, looked too much a gentleman to be accosted. They let him go on in silence across the small field to the wood.

There was not the least difference between this morning and those of the bright springs, six or eight years back. White and sandy-gold fowls still scratched round the gate, littering the earth and the field with feathers and scratched-up rubbish. Between the two thick holly bushes in the wood-hedge was the hidden gap, whose fence one climbed to get into the wood; the bars were scored just the same by the keeper's boots.

Syson was extraordinarily delighted. It is a wonderful thing, at twenty-nine, to have a Past. Like an emigrant he had returned, on a visit to the country of his past, to make comparison. The hazel still spread glad little hands downwards, the bluebells here were still wan and few, among the lush grass and in shade of the bushes.

The path through the wood, on the very brow of a slope, ran easily for a time. All around were twiggy oaks, just issuing their gold, and floor spaces diapered with woodruff, with patches of dog-mercury and tufts of hyacinth. The two fallen trees still lay across the track. Syson jolted down a steep, rough slope, and was again upon the open land, this time looking north as through a great window in the wood. He stayed to gaze over the level fields of the hill-top, at the village which strewed the bare upland plain as if it had tumbled off the passing waggons of civilisation, and been forsaken. There was a forlorn modern little grey church, and blocks and rows of red dwellings lying at random; at the back, the twinkling headstocks of the pit, and the looming pit-hill. All was naked and out-of-doors, not a tree! It was quite unaltered since his childhood.

Syson turned, satisfied, to follow the path that sheered downhill into the wood. He started. A keeper was standing a few yards in front, barring the way.

" Where might you be going this road, sir ? " asked the keeper. The man was inclined to be offensive. Syson looked at him with an artist's impersonal, observant gaze. The keeper was a young man of four or five and twenty, ruddy and comely. He had large, dark blue eyes, which now stared aggressively. His black moustache, very thick, was cropped short over a small, rather self-conscious, almost feminine mouth. In every other respect the man was unusually virile. He was just above middle height ; the strong forward thrust of his chest, and the perfect ease of his erect, proud carriage gave one the feeling that he was taut with life, like the thick jet of a fountain balanced at ease. He stood with the butt of his gun on the ground, staring insolently and questioningly at Syson. The dark, restless eyes of the trespasser, examining the man as if he were a tree or a flower, troubled the keeper and made him angry.

" Where's Naylor, and his velveteen skirts ? He can't be dead——? " Syson implored.

" You're not from the House, are you ? " inquired the keeper. It could not be, since everyone was away.

Syson's mobile mouth broke into a laugh.

" No, I'm not from the House," he said. It seemed to amuse him.

" Then are you going to answer my question ? " said the keeper disagreeably.

" Which ? Oh, certainly—I beg your pardon ! " Syson was laughing all the time. " I am going to Willey Water Farm."

" This isn't the road." The man was certainly a bully.

" I think so. Down this path, paddle through the water from the well, and out by the white gate. I could go blindfold."

" Happen so, but you'd be trespassing all the same, did you know that ? "

" Did I ? I say, how strange ! I am sorry. No, I used to come so often, in Naylor's time, I had forgotten. Where is he, by the way ?' '

" Crippled with rheumatism," the keeper answered reluctantly.

" I say ! " Syson exclaimed in pain.

" You'd happen tell me what your name is ? " asked the keeper, with a new intonation.

" John Adderley Syson, late of Cordy Lane."

" As used to court Hilda Millership ? "

Syson's eyes opened with a curious smile. He nodded. There was a very awkward silence.

" And you will introduce yourself ? " asked Syson.

" Arthur Pilbeam—Naylor's my uncle," said the other.

" You live here in Nuttall ? "

" I'm lodgin' at my uncle's—at Naylor's."

" I see ! "

" Did you say you was goin' down to Willey Water ? " asked the keeper.

" Yes."

" Well, at that rate I should like you to know—as *I'm* courtin' Hilda Millership."

The keeper looked at the intruder with a blaze of defiance, almost pitiful. Syson opened new eyes of astonishment.

" No-o ? " he cried, with incredulous irony. The keeper went scarlet to the ears. But :

" And she," he said, huffed, " is keeping company with me."

" Good God ! " exclaimed Syson. The other man waited uncomfortably.

" And is it a fixed thing between you ? " asked the intruder.

" What do you mean by that ? " retorted the other, sulkily.

" Well—does she—do you think of getting married before long ? "

It was evidently a sore point. The keeper kicked at a sod.

" We sh'd ha' been married afore now, if——" Pilbeam was full of resentment.

" Ah ! " Syson expressed his understanding in the monosyllable.

" I'm married myself," he added, after a time.

" You are ! " said the other, incredulously, with a touch of contempt.

Syson laughed in his brilliant, quick way.

" This last fifteen months," he said.

The keeper gazed at him with heavy, sulky, inscrutable gaze, apparently thinking back, and making connection.

" Why, what of it ? " asked Syson.

" Nothing," said the other sulkily, turning away.

There was silence for a moment.

" Ah well ! " said Syson, " I will leave you. I suppose you don't intend to turn me back." The keeper paid no attention. The two men stood high in an open space, grassy, set round with small sheaves of sturdy bluebells ; a little open platform on the brow of the hill. Syson took a few indecisive steps forward, then stopped.

" I say, how lovely ! " he cried.

He had come in full view of the downslope. The wide path ran from his feet like a river, and it was full of bluebells, save for a green winding thread down the centre, where the keeper walked. Like a stream the path opened into azure shallows at the levels, and there were pools of bluebells, with still the green thread winding through, like a thin current of ice-water through blue lakes. And from under the twig-purple of the bushes swam the shadowed blue, as if the flowers lay in flood water over the woodland.

" Ah, isn't it lovely ! " Syson exclaimed, a world of regret in his tones ; for this was his past, the country he had abandoned, in which he was now only a visitor. Wood pigeons cooed overhead, and the air was full of the brightness of myriad birds singing.

" If you're married, as you reckon you are, what do you keep writing to her for, and sending her all them poetry books and things ? " asked the keeper. Syson stared at him in astonishment for a time, then he began to smile :

" You see," he said, " I was not aware that she—that you . . ."

Again the keeper flushed scarlet.

" But if you reckon to be married——" he charged.

" Well—— ? " queried the other mockingly.

But, looking down the blue, beautiful path, Syson felt he had been wrong. " I have been keeping her—a sort of dog-in-the-manger," he said to himself. Aloud :

" She knows I'm married and all that," he said.

" What do you keep on with *her* for, then ? " urged the keeper.

" But why shouldn't I ? " Syson returned. He knew quite well. There was silence. Syson suddenly struck his thigh with his gloves, and drew himself up.

" Good-day," he said, bowing, very polite and distant. He strode off downhill. Now, everything seemed to him ironic : the two sallows, one all gold and perfume and murmur, one silver green and bristly, reminded him that here he had taught her about pollination. And now, in the paths sacred to their youth, he was walking under a smart of condemnation from a game-keeper, for interfering with the latter's girl.

" Ah well," he said to himself ; " the poor chap seems to have a grudge against me because she won't marry him. I'll do my best on his behalf." He grinned to himself, being in a very bad temper.

The farm was less than a hundred yards from the wood's edge. Almost, the wall of trees seemed to form the fourth side to the open quadrangle. The house faced the wood. With many pangs, Syson noted the plum-blossom falling on the daffodils and on the profuse, coloured primroses, which he himself had brought here and set. How they had increased ! There were thick tufts of scarlet, and pink, and pale purple primroses, under the plum-trees. He saw somebody glance at him through the kitchen window, heard men's voices.

The door opened suddenly : very womanly she had grown ! He felt himself going pale.

" You ?—Addy ! " she exclaimed, and stood motionless.

" Who ? " called the farmer's voice. Men's low voices answered. Those low voices, curious, and almost sneering, roused the ironic spirit in the visitor. Smiling brilliantly at her he bowed low :

" Myself—in all humility," he said.

The flush burned very deep on her cheek and throat.

" We are just finishing dinner," she said.

" Then I will stay outside." He made a motion to show that he would sit on the red earthenware pipkin that stood near the door among the daffodils, and contained the drinking water.

" Oh no, come in," she said hurriedly. He entered with reluctance. In the doorway, he glanced swiftly over the family, and bowed. Everyone was confused. The farmer, his wife, and the four sons sat at the coarsely laid dinner-table, the men with arms bare to the elbows.

" I am sorry I interrupt your lunch," said Syson.

" Don't mention it. Sit down and have a bit," said the farmer, trying to be free and easy.

" It's early for me," said Syson.

He noticed the women were uncomfortable, and would rather he did not accept.

" Why, what time *do* you reckon to have your dinner ? " asked Frank, the second son, insolently.

" Dinner ?—usually at half-past seven."

" Oh—ah—— ! " sneered the sons altogether.

They had once been intimate friends with this young man.

" We'll give Addy something when we've finished," said the mother, an invalid.

" Do not let me be any trouble. Lunch does not matter to me."

" He allus could live on fresh air an' scenery," laughed the youngest son, a lad of nineteen.

Syson went round the buildings, and into the orchard at the back of the house, where daffodils all along the hedgerow swung like yellow, ruffled birds on their perches. He loved the place extraordinarily, the hills ranging round, with bear-skin woods covering their giant shoulders, and small red farms like brooches clasping their garments ; the blue streak of water in the valley, the bareness of the pasture on the home-hills, the sound of myriad-threaded bird-song, which went mostly unheard. To his last day, he would dream of this place, when he felt the sun on his face, or saw the small handfuls of snow between the winter twigs.

Hilda was very womanly. In her presence, he felt boyish. She was twenty-nine, as he was, but she seemed to him much older. As he was fingering some shed plum-blossom on a low bough, she came to the back door to shake the tablecloth. Fowls raced from the stackyard, birds rustled from the trees. Her dark auburn hair was gathered up in a coil like a crown on her head. She was very straight, imperious in her bearing. As she folded the cloth, she looked away over the hills.

Presently Syson returned indoors. She had prepared eggs and curd cheese, stewed gooseberries and cream.

" Since you will dine to-night," she said, " I have only given you a light lunch."

" It is perfectly arcadian and delightful," he said. " I almost look for your belt of straw and ivy buds."

Still they mocked each other with irony. He knew it hurt her. But—she was courting the game-keeper and she should marry him.

In his private heart he was thinking, " What a woman she is—what a lot older she is ! " He was afraid of her now, seeing her so much altered. Her curt, sure speech, her proud, hard bearing, her reserve, were unfamiliar to him. He admired again her grey-black eyebrows, and her lashes ; he quarrelled with her set mouth, with the expressionless composure of her face. Their eyes met. He saw, in the beautiful grey and black of her glance, tears and bitterness, and at the back of all, calm acceptance of sorrow.

" She's much older than I," he said to himself. With an effort he kept up the ironic manner.

She sent him into the parlour while she washed the dishes. The long low room was refurnished from the Abbey sale, with chairs upholstered in claret-coloured rep, many years old, and an oval table of polished walnut, and a fresh piano, handsome, though still antique. In spite of the strangeness, he was pleased. Opening a high cupboard let into the thickness of the wall, he found it full of his books, his old lesson-books, and volumes of verse he had sent her, English and German. The daffodils in the white window-bottoms, shone across the room, he could almost feel their rays. The old glamour caught him again. His youthful watercolours on the walls no longer made him grin ; he remembered how fervently he had tried to paint for her, twelve years before.

She entered, wiping a dish, and he saw again the bright, kernel-white beauty of her arms.

" You are quite aristocratic here," he said, and their eyes met.

" Do you like it ? " she asked. It was the old, low, husky tone of intimacy. He felt a quick change beginning in his blood.

" Ay," he nodded, smiling at her like a boy again. She bowed her head.

" This was the countess's chair," she said in low tones. " I found her scissors down here between the padding."

" Ay— ! Show me."

Quickly, with a lilt in her movement, she fetched her work-basket, and together they examined the long-shanked old scissors.

" What a ballad of dead ladies ! " he said, laughing, as he fitted his fingers into the round loops of the countess's scissors.

" You are the only man who could use them," she said, with a little thrill. He looked at his fingers, and at the scissors :

" The only one of *your* men, perhaps," he said, putting the scissors aside with a sudden darkening in his soul. She turned to the window. He noticed the fine, fair down on her cheek and her upper lip, and her soft, white neck, like the throat of a nettle flower, and her fore-arms, bright as newly blanched kernels. She was being discovered afresh to him, who thought he knew her so thoroughly.

" Shall we go out awhile ? " she asked softly.

“ Ay ! ” he answered. But the predominant emotion, that flooded over the daring and the ecstasy in his heart, was fear. Something big was going to happen to him and to her, unless he took care, his soul warned him.

She put no covering on her head, merely took off her apron, saying : “ We will go by the larches.” As they passed the old orchard, she called him in to show him a blue-tit’s nest in one of the apple-trees, and a sycock’s in the hedge. He rather wondered at her surety, for she had been one to go dreamily unobservant.

“ Look at the apple buds,” she said, and he then perceived myriads of little scarlet balls among the drooping boughs. Watching his face, she laughed. He was dumb and stupid, and at the bottom, afraid. If he were going to fall in love with this old lover, whose youth had marched with his as stately, religious nights march beside reckless days, then it would be a love that would invade many lives and lay them waste. His soul realised this, not his reason. His mind was almost paralysed.

For her part, she was brilliant as he had not known her. She showed him nests : a jenny wren’s in a low bush.

“ See this jinty’s ! ” she exclaimed.

He was surprised to hear her use the local name. She reached carefully through the thorns, and put her finger in the nest’s round door.

“ Five ! ” she said. “ Teenty little things.”

She showed him nests of robins, and chaffinches, and linnets, and buntings ; of a wagtail beside the water :

“ And if we go down, nearer the lake, I will show you a kingfisher’s . . . .”

“ Among the young fir-trees,” she said, “ there’s a throstle’s or a blackie’s on nearly every shelf—hundreds. The first day, when I had seen them all, I felt as if I mustn’t go in the wood. It seemed a city of birds : and in the morning, hearing them all, I thought of the clamour of early markets. I was afraid to go in my own wood.”

The wasted poet in him did honour to her. He felt weak as water in her hands. She did not mind his silence, but was always a brilliant hostess entertaining him in her wood. As they came along a marshy path where forget-me-nots were opening in a rich blue drift :

" We know all the birds, but there are many flowers we can't find out,"—" I can't find out," she quickly corrected herself.

" We ? " he questioned.

She looked dreamily across to the open fields that slept in the sun :

" I have a lover as well, you know," she gently reprimanded him, dropping again into the intimate tone.

This woke in him the spirit of combat.

" I think I met him. He is very bonny—also in Arcady."

Without answering, she turned into a dark path that led up hill, where the trees and undergrowth were very thick.

" They did well," she said at length, " to have various altars to various gods, in old days."

" Ah yes ! " he agreed. " And which have you turned to now ? "

" Do you think I have left the old one ? " she asked, pathetically.

" No, not really. It was your highest, the one you kneeled at with me——"

" But *you* have left it," she said. He caught his breath, with a quick, painful frown.

" Ay—but the man doesn't matter so much," he said. There was a pause.

" And you are mistaken. I *have* turned away," she admitted, in a low, husky tone, averting her face from him.

There was silence, during which he pondered. The path was almost flowerless, gloomy. At the side, his heels sank into soft clay.

" No," she said, very slowly, " I was married the same night as you."

He looked at her a quick question.

" Not legally, of course," she replied, in the same grave, deliberate manner. " But—actually."

" ' Tandaradei,' " he mocked.

She turned to him brightly.

" You thought I could not ? " she said. But the flush was deep in her cheek and throat, for all her seeming assurance.

Still he would not say anything.

" You see,"—she was making an effort to explain—" *I* had to understand also, to keep pace."

To keep pace, she meant, with Syson, whom she loved with the deepest part of her nature.

" And does it amount to much, this *understanding ?* " he asked, cynically. She was shocked.

" A very great deal—does it not to you ? " she replied.

" And you are not disappointed ? "

" Far from it ! " Her tone was deep and sincere.

" Then you love him ? "

" Yes, I love him." She was tender, and gentle, in her thought of the keeper.

" Good ! " he said.

This silenced her for a while.

" Here, among his things, I do love him truly," she said.

His conceit would not let him be silent.

" And me ? " he asked, bitingly.

" So different ! " she cried.

He laughed shortly.

" You turned Opportunist ? " he said.

" 'Tis your doing," she replied.

For a moment the hearts of these two idealists stood still with despair.

They came to a place where the undergrowth shrank away, leaving a bare, brown space, pillared with the brick-red and purplish trunks of pine trees. On the fringe, was the sombre green of elder trees, with flat flowers in bud, and bright, unfurling pennons of fern. In the midst of the bare space stood a keeper's log hut. Pheasant-coops were lying about, some occupied by a clucking hen, some empty.

Hilda walked over the brown pine needles to the hut, took a key from among the eaves and opened the door. It was a bare wooden place with a carpenter's bench and form, carpenter's tools, an axe, snares, traps, some skins pegged down, everything in order. Hilda closed the door. Syson examined the weird flat coats of wild animals, that were pegged down to be cured. She pressed some knots of wood in the side wall, and an opening appeared in the bare logs, disclosing a second, small apartment.

" Is he a romantic, then ? " asked Syson, ponderingly.

" Perhaps so ! He is very curious—up to a certain point, cunning—in a nice sense—and inventive, and so thoughtful—but not beyond a certain point."

She pulled back a dark green curtain. The apartment was occupied almost entirely by a large couch of heather and bracken, on which was spread an ample rabbit-skin rug. On the floor were patchwork rugs of cat-skin, and a red calf-skin, while hanging from the wall were other furs. Hilda took down one, which she put on. It was a cloak of rabbit-skin edged with white fur, and with a hood, apparently of the skins of stoats. She laughed at Syson from out of this barbaric mantle, saying :

" What do you think of it ? "

" Ah—— ! I congratulate you on your man," he replied.

" And look ! " she said.

In a little jar on a shelf were some sprays, frail and white, of the first honeysuckle.

" They will scent the place at night," she said.

He looked round curiously.

" Then where does your keeper come short ? " he asked. She gazed at him for a few moments. Then, turning aside—

" The stars aren't the same with him," she said, intensely, " nor the forget-me-nots. You could make them flash and quiver, and the forget-me-nots come up at me like phosphorescence. I have found it out—it is true."

He laughed, saying :

" After all, stars and forget-me-nots are only luxuries."

" Ay," she assented sadly. " It is a pity."

Again he laughed quickly at her.

" Why ? " he asked, mockingly.

She turned swiftly. He was leaning against the small window of the tiny obscure room, and was watching her, who stood in the doorway, still cloaked in her mantle. His cap was removed, so she saw his face and head distinctly in the dim room. His black, straight, glossy hair was brushed clean back from his brow. His black eyes were playing a polite game with her, and his face, that was clear and cream, and perfectly smooth and healthy, was flickering with polite irony.

" You are very different," she said bitterly.

Again he laughed.

" I see you disapprove of me," he said.

" I disapprove of what you are becoming," she said.

" But you have still hopes of me ! Then what must I do to be—— "—he checked himself—" to avoid this calamity ? "

She saw that he was always laughing at her.

" If your own soul doesn't tell you, I cannot."

" I say," he cried, mock-serious, " where have I heard that before ? Besides," he continued politely, " one cannot live in Rome without being Romanised—unless one is fanatically patriotic —and really, you know, I am of no country."

" No—— ? " she said bitterly.

" Unless I have been adopted unaware." That, he felt, was insulting, and his spirit turned in shame.

" You are a Roman of the Romans," she said sarcastically.

" Of the emasculated period," he laughed. " But 'twas you would have it so."

" I ! " she exclaimed.

" You *would* have me take the Grammar School scholarship—and you would have me foster poor little Botell's fervent attachment to me, till he couldn't live without me—and because Botell was rich and influential. You insisted on my accepting the wine-merchant's offer to send me to Cambridge, there to chaperon his only child. Then you bade me go into the business until I had money—and then—and then——; well, ' Now ' is the realisation. I have done exceedingly well, for an orphan son of a village schoolmaster."

" And I am responsible ? " she asked, with sarcasm.

" I was a most plastic youth," he laughed.

" Ah," she cried, " I sent you away too young."

" But I am a *great* success—and really, I enjoy it. You keep preaching me the ' Tongues in trees ' business, and ' good in everything ' that is not London. But I assure you, there's quite a lot to be said for my side. ' I would not change it.' "

" You are too glib," she said, in very cutting tones.

" I always had that defect," he said, bowing.

There was a rattling at the outer latch, and the keeper entered. The woman glanced round, but remained standing, fur-cloaked, in the inner doorway. Syson, quite indifferent, did not move.

The keeper entered, saw, and turned away without speaking. The others also were silent.

Pilbeam attended to his skins.

" Have we finished our duel ? " asked Syson.

" I have nothing more to say," she replied.

" Then I give you ' To our vast and varying fortunes.' " He lifted his hand in pledge.

" ' To our vast and varying fortunes,' " she answered, bowing gravely, and speaking in cold tones.

" Arthur ! " she said.

The keeper pretended not to hear. Syson, watching keenly, began to smile. The woman drew herself up.

" Arthur ! " she said again, with a curious upward inflection, which warned the two men that her soul was trembling on one of those sudden changes that are so striking in women ; as when a drop of acid suddenly throws out a black, turbid precipitate in a clear liquid.

The keeper slowly put down his tool and came to her.

" Yes," he said.

" I wanted to introduce you," she said, cold and deliberate.

" I know him—I've met him before," growled the keeper.

" Never mind—I want to introduce you formally. Addy, Mr. Pilbeam, to whom I am engaged to be married. Arthur—Mr. Syson, who was an old friend of ours." Syson bowed, but the other mechanically held out his hand. The two men shook hands.

" Allow me to congratulate you heartily," said Syson. In his heart he was saying bitterly, " Mrs. Pilbeam—Good God ! "

He bade the woman good-bye.

" Which way will you go ? " she asked.

" Over Foster's," he replied.

" Arthur, you will go with Mr. Syson to the gate," she said. They went all three together down the gloomy path.

" Ah les beaux jours dė bonheur indicible
Où nous joignions nos bouches . . . "

quoted Syson, half-sincere, half-mocking.

" C'est possible ! " she replied, in the same spirit.

" Good ! " he cried. " We might have rehearsed it. I never could help being sentimental. How does it go on ?

' Qu'il etait bleu, le ciel, et grand l'espoir.' "

" I never liked farce," she replied, cuttingly. " Besides, *we* cannot walk in *our* wild oats. You were too modest and good to sow any at that time."

Syson looked at her. He was shocked that she could sneer at their young love, which had been the greatest thing he had known. Certainly he had killed her love at last, as he had often wished he could. Now he felt a great sense of desolation.

At the bottom of the path she left him. As he went along with the keeper, towards the open, he said :

" You will let me know when you are going to be married, will you ? "

" Why ? " asked the keeper.

" Because she will not write to me—at least till after—I know."

" Well—— ! " said the keeper, disagreeably, but hesitating.

" I shan't be in Nuttall again for years—perhaps never. I shall want to know your news, for all that. So if you'll write to me, I will write to you. All the correspondence shall be between us two."

He handed the young keeper his card.

" All right then—we'll let it stand at that."

They were at the gate. Syson held out his hand. When he was a dozen yards across the field, the other called :

" I say, I s'll only write when there's something definite."

" Quite so ! " said Syson, and each turned his several way.

Instead of going straight to the high road gate, Syson went along the wood's edge, where the brook spread out in a little bog, and under the alder trees, among the reeds, great yellow stools and bosses of marigolds shone. Threads of brown water trickled by, touched with gold from the flowers. Suddenly, there was a blue flash in the air, as a kingfisher passed.

Syson was extraordinarily wretched. He climbed the bank to the gorse bushes, whose sparks of blossom had not yet gathered into a flame. Lying on the dry brown turf, he discovered sprigs of tiny purple milkwort and pink spots of lousewort. He began to count his losses. In spite of himself, he was unutterably miserable, though not regretful. He would not alter what he had done. Yet he was drearily, hopelessly wretched. After a while he had got it clear.

" She always knew the best of me, and believed in the best I might be. Whilst she kept her ideal ' Me ' living, I was sort of responsible to her : I must live somewhere up to standard. Now

I have destroyed Myself in her, and I am alone, my star is gone out. I have destroyed the beautiful ' Me ' who was always ahead of me, nearer the realities. And I have struck the topmost flower from off her faith. And yet it was the only thing to do, considering all the other folk . . . "

He lay quite still, feeling a kind of death.

Presently he heard voices : the keeper was coming down the path, with his wife.

" Say what ails thee ? " Syson heard the keeper ask gently, but with a touch of resentment.

" I am a bit upset—don't bother me," pleaded the woman.

Syson turned over. The air was full of the sound of larks, as if the sunshine above were condensing and falling in a shower. Amid this bright sound, the voices sounded like horn-music.

" Yes, but what upsets thee," persisted the man.

" Go home now, Arthur. I will talk to you to-night."

Syson looked through the bushes. Hilda was leaning on the gate, tears running down her face. The man was in the field, loitering by the hedge, and, Syson at last made out, was catching the bees as they settled on the white bramble flowers, crushing them in his palm, and letting them fall, not aware what he was doing.

There was silence for a while, in which Syson imagined her tears among the brightness of the larks. Suddenly the keeper exclaimed " Ah ! " and swore loudly. He was gripping at the sleeve of his coat, near the shoulder. Then he pulled off his jacket, threw it on the ground, and absorbedly rolled up his shirt sleeve right to the shoulder.

" Ah ! " he said vindictively, as he picked out the bee and flung it away. He twisted his fine, bright arm, peering awkwardly over his shoulder.

" What is it ? " asked Hilda quietly.

" A bee—crawled up my sleeve and stung me," he answered.

" Come here to me," she said.

The keeper went to her, like a sulky boy. She took his handsome arm in her hands.

" Here it is—and the sting left in—poor bee ! "

She picked out the sting, put her mouth to his arm, and sucked away the drop of poison. As she looked at the red mark her mouth had made, and at his arm, she said, laughing winsomely out of her tears :

" That is the reddest kiss you will ever have."

He put his arms round her, and was kissing her. When Syson next looked up, at the sound of voices, he saw the keeper with his mouth on the throat of his beloved, whose head was thrown back, and whose hair had fallen, so that one rough rope of dark brown hair hung across his bare arm.

" No," the woman answered. " I am not upset because he's gone. You won't understand. . . . ."

Syson could not distinguish what the man said. Hilda replied, clear and distinct :

" You know I love you. He has gone quite out of my life—I don't know what I should do without you . . . ." She ended plaintively. He kissed her warmly, murmuring. She laughed quickly.

" Yes," she said indulgent, but slightly bitter. " We will be married, we will be married. You can tell people, and make arrangements." He embraced her again. Syson heard nothing for a time. Then she said :

" You must go home, now, dear—you will get no sleep."

" Shall we be married at church, or chapel or what—— ? "

" We will be married at church."

It was the first time she had used the plural pronoun in that way, which moved the keeper to embrace her fervently. At last he pulled on his coat and departed. She stood at the gate, not watching him, but looking south over the sunny counties towards London, far away.

When at last she had gone, Syson also departed, going south.

THE BEGGAR'S HUNT By W. H. DAVIES

WE have no mind to reach that Pole
  Where monarchs keep their icy courts ;
Where lords and ladies, proud and cold,
  May do no more than smile at sports ;
Nay, laughing, lying at our ease,
  We keep our court beneath green trees.

Kings' beds are soft and silvery white,
  But ours are golden straw or hay ;
So let kings lie while gentle sleep
  Attends our harder beds, when they
Inside their soft, white bedclothes yell
That nightmares ride them down to hell.

Poor lords and ladies, what tame sport
  To hunt a fox or stag, while we
Sit on a green bank in the sun,
  And chase for hours a faster flea ;
Which blesses us from day to day,
With all our faculties in play.

I had been resting for a little time and, as I was about to continue my journey, I looked back and saw a man in the distance, coming towards me. Seeing that he was going my way, I settled down again, to wait for him, watching his movements as he came along. I noticed at once that he was walking at a fast pace, but what surprised me was that he often came to a halt and made his hands feel various parts of his clothes. My first impression was that he had lost something and was searching for it. I saw him halt quite a number of times and make these quick movements, feeling down both his legs, then in his bosom, and sometimes up both his sleeves. " The poor fellow is in a terrible state of worry," thought I ; " perhaps he has lost silver, or even gold, which has been his savings. Such a loss would be almost madness to a poor looking man like that." However, these thoughts did not last long, for I soon came to the conclusion that the man was scratching himself, owing to the attack of fleas.

When he reached my side, I saw at once that he was inclined to pass on without saying a word, but I brought him to a halt by inquiring his destination for the day. He did not answer for some time, for he had put his hand down the back of his neck to scratch his shoulder blade, and this action choked his utterance. As soon as he was able to speak he answered that he was on his way to Hungerford. " Let us walk together for a little way," I said, " for I am going there too. But I am not able to walk very fast." Saying this I gave him twopence, knowing that he would be in no hurry after that, as he would hope for further kindness before we parted for good. To encourage him in this belief, I offered him tobacco, at the same time saying—" I shall be glad when we come to an inn." He began to scratch more than ever now, as much from delight as from fleas.

" Are you out of work ? " I asked, as we went along. " I am," he answered ; " there is no work to be had anywhere. Curse it." Saying this he began to scratch his left shoulder, and I knew at once that it was a flea, and not the lack of work, that was the object of his curse. " Have you been out of work long ? " I inquired. " Two months," he answered ; " and I never expect to be in work again. Curse it ! " This time he began to scratch his left thigh, and I again came to the conclusion that a flea, and not the lack of work, was the reason why he swore. Of course, I could see plainly that this man was a tramp of a very long standing, who did not trouble his head about work, but would not let me know the truth.

We went on like this for about half a mile, talking of the difficulties of a man out of work, which my ragged companion said were " heart-breaking." " Yes," he said, coming to a halt, and beginning to scratch under his right arm—" Yes, this kind of life is heart-breaking. Curse it ! "

At last I saw a signboard not far away, and knew it was an inn.

But by this time I began to have my doubts as to the wisdom of having this man's company, even in the very lowest kind of a tavern ; where the landlord or his customers would be certain to object to his company. However, I did not like to let him go without first giving him a glass of beer. So I came to a halt and said, " We will go into this inn, but while we are there, can you stop scratching ? " " Of course I can," he answered readily, as though nothing in the world was easier. " You must understand," I continued, " that the landlord, or his wife, or his daughter, whichever serves us, would not care to have a customer that kept on scratching himself. So, drink and laugh, but, for God's sake, don't scratch ! " When my ragged companion heard this he laughed heartily and began to scratch himself all over. When I saw his delight, I could not help laughing as heartily myself. However, after his glee was over, I said kindly, so as not to hurt his feelings, " You'll try not to scratch, won't you ? " When I had done speaking, my companion, who had been motionless for quite half a minute, said in slow, distinct tones—" If I *say* I won't scratch, I *won't* scratch. And if I do, may the devil pickle and purge me ! "

With this understanding we made our way towards the inn. But we had scarcely gone ten steps when my companion waved his hand with a wide sweep, saying—" This is a beautiful county !" When I heard this, I at once had a suspicion that something was wrong. So, although I looked away from him for a moment, I turned quickly in his direction and was just in time to catch him in the act of scratching his right leg. Seeing this I made up my mind to enter the inn alone. So I took threepence out of my pocket and said—" Do what you like now, for I shall probably be at this inn for a couple of hours. Good-bye." " Thank you," he answered, grasping my hand, " you're a true gentleman. Good-bye and good luck." Saying this he went off with all speed.

When I entered the inn, which was called the Waggon and Horses, I saw my late companion sitting in the taproom, with a glass of beer in his hand. Whether the landlady had been civil to him or not, I cannot say, but it was most certain that when I entered she cast several cold glances at her other customer. However, the latter appeared to take little heed of this, and sat with his two arms leaning on the table. It must not be inferred from this attitude that he was not scratching. There he sat, his arms motionless, it is true, but what about his feet ? If the landlady, who had now retired, could have seen those feet, as they were seen by me, she would have ordered him out of her house at once. For there he sat, resting on one leg at a time, while the foot of the other leg was kept busy scratching. But this secret method was not satisfying for long, for in a few moments he gave his feet a rest and set his hands to work on the upper parts of his body. After doing this for a short time, he suddenly got up, finished his beer and ran headlong out of the house.

After having had some bread and cheese and pickles, some beer, and a rest of half an hour, I left the Waggon and Horses and continued my journey towards Hungerford. But I had not been walking more than twenty minutes when I heard a voice hail me from behind a steep bank. When I looked, I saw my late companion. " Wait a minute," he cried, " for I am now ready to travel." " Have you been sleeping ? " I asked, when he had reached my side. " No," he answered with a laugh, " I have been having a lively time at hunting and killing fleas. I shall sleep well after this excitement."

As we walked along he talked of nothing but hunting and killing fleas, saying that hunting hares, foxes or stags was but poor sport compared with that. The subject seemed to interest him so much that he could not change to another and was still at it when we were within a short distance of Hungerford.

THE ESPERANTO OF ART By W. L. GEORGE

IT is established and accepted to-day that a painter may not like music, that a writer may yawn in a picture-gallery: though we proclaim that art is universal, it certainly is not universal for the universe. This should not surprise us who know that van Gogh wrote: " To paint and to love women is incompatible "; van Gogh was right for himself, which does not mean that he was right for everybody, and I will not draw from his dictum the probably incorrect conclusion that " To paint and to love literature is incompatible." But van Gogh, who had not read Bergson, was indicating clearly enough that he knew he must canalise his powers, therefore exclude from his emotional purview all things which did not appertain directly to his own form of art.

Form of art! Those three words hold the difficulty of mutual understanding among artists. While sympathising with van Gogh in his xenophobia, I cannot accept that because certain artists could not appreciate certain forms of art, no artist can understand another whose form is alien to him. There is, there must be a link between the painter, the sculptor, the writer, the musician, the actor, between the poet in words and the one, to-day most common, who wishes to express himself in the deeds of his own life. For art is, we are assured thereof, all of one stuff. A symphony and a poem may be allotropic forms of the same matter: to use a common simile, there is red phosphorus and there is yellow, but both are phosphorus. Likewise there are different forms of art, as there are three Incomprehensibles, but there is only one art, as there is but one Incomprehensible.

It is important that artists should understand one another so that conflict may arise from their impressions, so that they may form a critical brotherhood. Some, to-day, are able to grasp one another's meaning and yet find it difficult, because every form of art has its own jargon, to express what they mean; they can grasp that the painter equally with the writer is striving to express himself, but they fail to phrase their appreciation and their criticism because writers cannot talk of masses or painters of style. There stands between them a hedge of technique; so thick is it that often they cannot see the soul of the works; their difficulty is one of terms. Now I do not suggest that the musician should study Praxiteles and himself carve marble; he is better employed expressing his own passion in the Key of C. But I do feel that if technical terms are the preserve of each form of art, general terms are not; that *continuity*, *rhythm*, *harmony*, to quote but a few, have a precise meaning, that they are inherent to no form of art because they are inherent to art itself.

The following, then, is a forlorn attempt to find the common language, the esperanto of art. It is made up of general terms (in italics); it represents no more than a personal point of view, and is for this reason laid down in a tentative spirit: it is not a solution but a fingerpost. Order being a necessary antidote for the abstruse, I have divided the terms into groups, according to their nature, to the dimension they affect or the matter to which they refer. Following this line of thought we find that works of art affect us in virtue of four properties: their power, their logic, their movement, and their attitude; this leads us to four groups of properties:

Group A. (Volumetric): *Concentration*, *Relief*, *Density*, *Depth*.

Group B. (Linear): *Linking*, *Continuity*.

Group C. (Kinetic): *Rhythm*, *Intensity*, *Reaction*, *Key*, *Culmination*.

Group D. (Static): *Grace*, *Balance*, *Harmony*.

This is a rough classification, for an opera does not necessarily compare with a square rood of paint or a novel of Tolstoyan length; indeed, on the volumetric basis, an opera may have less bulk than a sonnet.

Group A. (Volumetric). By *concentration* we mean the quality of conveying a great deal within a small space. It follows that *concentration* is in inverse ratio to area, though it does not follow that area is in inverse ratio to *concentration*. While "Anna Karenin" is an enormous novel it is as concentrated as the sonnet of d'Arvers ; on the other hand, Francis Thompson's "Arab Love Song" is more concentrated than the complete works of Mrs. Henry Wood ; while any Rubens is more concentrated than a modern miniature, an intaglio may be more concentrated than twenty square yards of Delacroix. We nullify areas, therefore, and must lay down that the test of concentration is the effect : if the painter realises that the author has felt all he wrote, if the writer sees that every line was necessary, then both can be sure that they are respectively in presence of concentrated works.

Likewise with *relief*. A bas-relief may have none. A fresco may. *Relief* then is a matter of contrast, as is shown especially in the mosaics of Taj Mahal ; but its nature is easily seen if we compare prose with paint :

" He stood at the edge of the sea while the waves crept towards him, nearer and nearer, sinuously flowing and ebbing, but ever nearer. Ever."

I give this as an instance, not as a fragment of literature. The lonely " ever " gives *relief* to the sentence of twenty-four words if we assume that another long sentence follows. (If no sentence follows, " ever " is no longer *relief* but *culmination*, see Group C.) The painter renders the same effect by a more vivid line of foam in the middle distance, the musician by interposing a treble motif between basses. Thus, if we find variety of sentence, variety of tone we have *relief*.

Density and *Depth* need not detain us long. Flaubert, the Psalms, the Eroica and Velasquez all give the sensation we call by those names ; we mean by them that each contains a suggestion of something behind. Atmospheric quality, then, together with thought withdrawn, echo unheard and space unlimned, are the bases on which the two terms rest. The suggestion that this " behind " exists is of course essential, for we must not conclude that where there is nothing to be seen there is something to be guessed : there must be no guessing, but if a feeling of reserve is created then *density* and *depth* exist.

Group B. (Linear). The quality of *linking* is opposed to the quality of discord, though a discord may prove to be a link. The most perfect instances of *linking* and *continuity*, for I almost identify the terms, are the solar spectrum and the song of the lark, but in the field of art we must be content with the gamut, the sequence of shades and the concatenation of phrases. In prose :

" The bird rose up into the air, and its wings beat slowly. The air was laden with mist. The bird rose towards the clouds . ." is an instance where there is a solution of continuity, which could be remedied if the second sentence were related to the flight of the bird. And the same lack of continuity would exist if the painter of a harlequin were to make his skull-cap brown, if in a pause of some work of Locatelli the musician interposed (however skilfully and gradually) some characteristic Grieg chords.

It does not, of course, follow that a discord is discontinuous. Providing it recurs within the scheme of the work, as the clashes in " Elektra," the sequence of discords becomes a sequence of links, and we arrive at this paradox, that it is the solutions of continuity provide the continuity, while the apparently continuous portions of the work are carried by the discordant sections. Thus there is continuity in the Louvre Ghirlandajo because equivalent, if minor, discords repeat the motif of the red mantle in two other portions of the picture. The relation of the discords is sometimes vital to more than continuity, namely to *rhythm* (Group C.).

With Group C. (Kinetic) we touch the most vital portion of the subject, for the kinetic quality in art amounts to the quality of life in man. And its chief component is *rhythm*. If *rhythm* be taken as a condition of internal movement within the inanimate, as a suggestion of expanding and retracting life, of phrases (musical, pictorial or literary) that come to an inevitable resolution, it is seen that its presence in a work of art must baffle until it is realised under what guise it appears. A simple instance of prose rhythm is :

" The wayfarer stopped by the well. He looked within its

depths and the water was far below. Idly he dropped a pebble between the walls; and it seemed minutes while he waited until the water sped its thanks."

This is not metrical but rhythmic prose, and it would be wearisome if the rhythm were not altered from paragraph to paragraph; short sentences alternate with long at fixed intervals, or passive verbs are inset between actives, while Gothic words juxtaposed to Latin, or adjectival combinations, produce the same effect of rise and fall. The rhythm may be regular as the movement of a woman's breast or spasmodic within the regular as the flight of a gull.

Pictorially *rhythm* is best gauged by certain tapestries based on the flower backgrounds of Fergusson and Anne Estelle Rice. Assume a black square of cloth; if the flowers are grouped thus, from left to right: dark red, pink, white, there is no rhythm, for the mental line is a mere downgrade; if they are grouped: dark red, light blue, dark green, there is no rhythm, for the mental line is a mere curve, a circular or perhaps parabolic basin; but if the grouping amounts to: dark red, pink, light blue, black, light green, cream, dark brown, there is a sensation of ebb and flow, rise and fall, *rhythm*. And this applies to drawing also, if we accept that colour is indicated by line, that lines are colours and that colours are tenses. That line can indicate colour is beyond denial, for we accept that colour is not material while tone is material. Colour being the relation of an impression to the impression of colourlessness, and tone being the resultant translation of the intensity of the colour, then it is feasible to reproduce a red and blue combination by a green and yellow combination of equal contrast. Therefore a combination of blacks may be made to balance a combination of even seven colours, provided the relative intensity (amount) of the blacks is in a true relation, in tone, with the relative intensity of the colours.

The quality of *rhythm* being absolutely obvious in music needs no discussion; it is the only form of rhythm the popular can recognise, but if we accept the principles of grouping in phrase and colour, no musician will fail to recognise a sarabande in the dance of Matisse or in the posturings of Kellermann's clown.

As for *intensity*, with which goes *reaction*, for the first cannot exist without the second, it is naturally brought about by the rhythmic focussing of the subject's attention upon words, colours or notes. Intensity is marked, for instance, by the triplets of the Venusberg music, their continual, slow billowing; it can be found, less easily, in phrases and colours, but it must exist if the work is art. In prose it is marked by a general nervousness of form and word:

" Upon the crag the tower pointed to the sky like a finger of stone, and about its base were thick bushes, which had burst forth into flower patches of purple and scarlet. The air was heavy with their scent."

Here the *intensity* is confined within the simile and the colour scheme ; the intervening space corresponds to the background of a picture, while the final short sentence, purposely dulled, is the *reaction*. Evidently (and all the more so as I have chosen a pictorial effect) an analogous intensity could be obtained in a painting : the flower patches could be exaggerated in colour to the uttermost limit of the palette, while the reagent final sentence was figured by a filmy treatment of the atmosphere. The limit to *intensity* is the *key* in which the work is conceived. But the word *key* must not be taken in its purely musical sense ; obviously, within the same piece the governing motif must not be andante at the beginning and presto at the end, but in artistic generalisations it must be taken as the spirit that informs rather than as the technical rule which controls. Thus, in literature, the *key* is the attitude of the writer : if in one part of the book his thought recalls Thackeray and in another Paul de Kock the *key* has been changed ; and again if the left side of the picture is pointillist, the right side cubist, the *key* has been changed. I choose exaggerated, almost absurd instances to make the point clear ; in practice, when the writer, the musician or the painter appears to have seen consistently, the key he has worked in is steadfast.

It should be said that uniformity of *key* does not imply absence of *reaction :* there is room, while the *key* remains uniform, for the juxtaposition of burlesque and romance, just as there is room in Holbein's " Ambassadors " for the incomprehensible object in the foreground, said to be a pun (Hohl Bein). But the *key* needs to be kept in mind as its maximum expression is the *culmination* of the effect. The *culmination* of a speech is in its peroration ; of a poem in its incorporated envoi. Thus in the " Arab Love Song," the *culmination* is :

" And thou what needest with thy tribe's black tents
Who hast the red pavilion of my heart ? "

There is no difficulty there. But in painting the *culmination* is more subtle. It consists in the isolation of the chief object. Say that we have from left to right : Black, yellow, dark brown, light blue, dark red " ; then add on the extreme right crimson, then gold. The picture *culminates* on the extreme right, with the result that attention is directed there and that any object in that section of the picture benefits by an influence about equivalent to that of footlights. *Culmination* involves the painter in great difficulties, for there must be *culmination*, while an effect in the wrong place may destroy the *balance* of his work. This appertains to

Group D. (Static). Its chief quality, *balance*, is easily defined in painting. Where there is correspondence between every section of the picture, where no value is exaggerated, *balance* exists. Hence the failure of Futurism. While the Futurists understand very well *intensity*, *reaction* and *relief*, they refuse to give *balance* any attention at all ; leaving aside the absurdity of rendering the mental into terms of the pictorial, and taking as an instance one who was once less Futurist than the Futurists, Severini, we see in his " Pan-pan Dance " how he detached himself from his school : he attained *balance* by giving every object an equal *intensity*. Evidently if there are no clashes of tone-values there must be *balance*, and the instance serves to show that where there are clashes of tone-values *balance* must be ensured by the artist's hand. There is always *balance* in the purely decorative; in the realistic there is *balance* if the attention of the beholder is directed simultaneously to the several points of *culmination* indicated by the *rhythm* of the picture. Thus there is *balance* in Rothenstein's " Chloe " because the rocks on the right repeat the significance of the rocks on the left.

Likewise in literature there is balance in certain groupings of phrases:

" The waves rolled in. Every one, edged with foam, curved forward to kiss the sand. Silvery in the sun they rolled. And they came assured, as if they had forgotten that they had come at other dawns, only to retire before the inert earth."

This is almost the exact " short-long-short-long " of waves themselves, and there is *balance* because each short-long grouping figures one curled wave. Nothing clarifies this idea so well as the Morse Code.

With perfect *balance* go *grace* and *harmony*. While *grace* must stand by itself as a not especially important quality because it is not, need not, always be present, *harmony* must be recognised as a synonym of *balance*. It is only because *grace* is often used where *harmony* is meant that it finds a place in this glossary. Obviously there is no *grace* in Rodin's Balzac, while there is *grace* in every note of Lulli and Glück; by *grace* we mean the quality of lightness we find in Pater, Meredith, André Gide, Mozart, Watteau, Donatello: the instances suffice to indicate the meaning, while *harmony*, if it be taken as a synonym of *balance* needs no further explanation than has been given for that term.

I venture to repeat in conclusion that there is nothing dogmatic about these ideas. They are subject to criticism and objection, for we are groping in the dark towards what Mr. Leonard Inkster calls the standardisation of artistic terms; if I prefer to his scientific way the more inspired suggestion of " esperanto," that is a common language of the arts, it is without fear of being called metaphysical. It may be argued that a purely intellectual attempt to extract and correlate the inspirations of forms of art is a metaphysical exercise doomed to failure by its own ambition. I do not think so. For art is universal enough to contain all the appeals, the sensuous, the intellectual and, for those who perceive it, the spiritual ; but the sensuous is incapable of explanation because sensuousness is a thing of perceptions which vanish as soon as the brain attempts to state them in mental terms ; and the spiritual, which I will define much as I would faith as a stimulation produced by a thing which one knows to be inexistent, also resists analysis ; if we are to bridge the gulf that separates the various forms of art, some intellectual process must be applied. Now it may be metaphysical to treat of the soul in terms of the intellect, but the intellect has never in philosophic matters refrained from laying hands upon the alleged soul of man ; I see no reason, therefore, to place art higher than the essence of human life and grant it immunity from attack and exegesis by the intellect. Indeed, the intellect in its metaphysical moods is alone capable of solving the riddle of artistic sensation. Once defined by intellect and applied by intellect, the esperanto of the arts may well serve to reconcile them and demonstrate to their various forms, against their will, their fundamental unity.

EPILOGUE: PENSION SEGUIN By KATHERINE MANSFIELD

THE servant who opened the door was twin sister to that efficient and hideous creature bearing a soup tureen into the *First French Picture*. Her round red face shone like freshly washed china. She had a pair of immense bare arms to match, and a quantity of mottled hair arranged in a sort of bow. I stammered in a ridiculous, breathless fashion, as though a pack of Russian wolves were behind me rather than five flights of beautifully polished French stairs. " Have you a room? " The servant girl did not know. She would ask Madame. Madame was at dinner. " Will you come in, please ? " Through the dark hall, guarded by a large black stove that had the appearance of a headless cat with one red all-seeing eye in the middle of its stomach, I followed her into the salon. " Please to sit down," said the servant girl, closing the door behind her. I heard her list slippers shuffle along the corridor, the sound of another door opening—a little clamour—instantly suppressed. Silence followed. The salon was long and narrow, with a yellow floor dotted with white mats. White muslin curtains hid the windows : the walls were white, decorated with pictures of pale ladies drifting down cypress avenues to forsaken temples, and moons rising over boundless oceans. You would have thought that all the long years of Madame's virginity had been devoted to the making of white mats—that her childish voice had lisped its numbers in crochet work stitches. I did not dare to begin counting them. They rained upon me from every possible place, like impossible snowflakes. Even the piano stool was buttoned into one embroidered with *P. F.* I had been looking for a resting place all the morning. At the start I flew up innumerable stairs as though they were major scales—the most cheerful things in the world—but after repeated failures the scales had resolved into the minor, and my heart which was quite cast down by this time, leapt up again at these signs and tokens of virtue and sobriety. " A woman with such sober passions," thought I, " is bound to be quiet and clean, with few babies and a much absent husband. Mats are not the sort of things that lend themselves in their making to cheerful singing. Mats are essentially the fruits of pious solitude. I shall certainly take a room here." And I began to dream of unpacking my clothes in a little white room, and getting into a kimono and lying on a white bed, watching the curtains float out from the window in the delicious autumn air that smelled of apples and honey . . . until the door opened and a tall thin woman in a lilac pinafore came in, smiling in a vague fashion. " Madame Seguin ? " " Yes, Madame." I repeated the familiar story. A quiet room. Removed from any church bells, or crowing cocks, or little boys' schools, or railway stations. " There are none of such things anywhere near here," said Madame, looking very surprised. " I have a very beautiful room to let, and quite unexpectedly. It has been occupied by a young gentleman from Buenos Ayres whose father died, unfortunately, and implored him to return home immediately. Quite natural, indeed." " Oh, very ! " said I, hoping that the Hamlet-like apparition was at rest again and would not invade my solitude to make certain of his son's obedience. "If Madame will follow me." Down a dark corridor, round a corner I felt my way. I wanted to ask Madame if this was where Buenos Ayres père appeared unto his son, but I did not dare to. " Here—you see. Quite away from everything," said Madame.

I have always viewed with a proper amount of respect and abhorrence those penetrating spirits who are not susceptible to appearances. What is there to believe in except appearances ? I have nearly always found that they are the only things worth enjoying at all, and if ever an innocent child lays its head upon my knee and begs for the truth of the matter, I shall tell it the story of my one and only nurse, who, knowing my horror of gooseberry jam, spread a coating of apricot over the top of the jam jar. As long as I believed it apricot I was happy, and learning wisdom, I contrived to eat the apricot and leave the gooseberry behind. " So, you see, my little innocent creature," I shall end, " the great thing to learn in this life is to be content with appearances, and shun the vulgarities of the grocer and the philosopher."

Bright sunlight streamed through the windows of the delightful room. There was an alcove for the bed, a writing table was placed against the window, a couch against the wall. And outside the window I looked down upon an avenue of gold and red trees and up at a range of mountains white with fresh fallen snow. " One hundred and eighty francs a month," murmured Madame, smiling at nothing, but seeming to imply by her manner " of course this has nothing to do with the matter." I said, " That is too much. I cannot afford more than one hundred and fifty francs." " But," explained Madame, " the size ! the alcove. And the extreme rarity of being overlooked by so many mountains." " Yes," I said. " And then the food. There are four meals a day, and breakfast in your room if you wish it." " Yes," I said, more feebly. " And my husband a professor at the Conservatoire—that again is so rare." Courage is like a disobedient dog. Once it starts running away, it flies all the faster for your attempts to recall it. " One hundred and sixty," I said. " If you agree to take it for two months I will accept," said Madame very quickly. I agreed.

Marie helped to unstrap my boxes. She knelt on the floor, grinning and scratching her big red arms.

" Ah, how glad I am Madame has come," she said. " Now we shall have some life again. Monsieur Arthur, who lived in this room—he was a gay one. Singing all day, and sometimes dancing. Many a time Mademoiselle Ambatielos would be playing and he'd dance for an hour without stopping." " Who is Mademoiselle Ambatielos ? " I asked. " A young lady, studying at the Conservatoire," said Marie, sniffing in a very friendly fashion. " But she gives lessons, too. Ah, mon Dieu, sometimes when I'm dusting her room I think her fingers will drop off. She plays all day long. But I like that—that's life, noise is. That's what I say. You'll hear her soon. Up and down she goes ! " said Marie, with extreme heartiness. " But," I cried, loathing Marie, " how many other people are staying here ? " Marie shrugged. " Nobody to speak of. There's the Russian gentleman, a priest he is, and Madame's three children—and that's all. The children are lively enough," she said, filling the washstand pitcher, " but then, there's the baby—the boy! Ah, you'll know about him, poor little one, soon enough ! " She was so detestable, I would not ask her anything further.

I waited until she had gone, and leaned against the window-sill, watching the sun deepen in the trees until they seemed full and trembling with gold, and wondering what was the matter with the mysterious baby.

All through the afternoon Mademoiselle Ambatielos and the piano warred with the Appassionata Sonata. They shattered it to bits and remade it to their heart's desire—they unpicked it—and tried it in various styles. They added a little touch—caught up something. Finally they decided that the only thing of importance was the loud pedal. The mysterious baby, hidden behind Heaven knows how many doors, cried with such curious persistence that I had to strain my ears, wondering if it was a baby or an engine or a far-off whistle. At dusk Marie, accompanied by the two little girls, brought me a lamp. My appearance disturbed these charming children to such an extent that they rushed up and down the corridor in a frenzied state for half an hour afterwards, bumping themselves against the walls, and shrieking with derisive laughter. At eight the gong sounded for supper. I was hungry. The corridor was filled with the warm, strong smell of cooked meat. " Well," I thought, " at any rate, judging by the smell the food must be good." And feeling very frightened I entered the dining room.

Two rows of faces turned to watch me. M. Seguin introduced me, rapped on the table with the soup spoon, and the two little girls, impudent and scornful, cried " Bon soir, Madame," while the baby, half washed away by his afternoon performance, emptied his cup of milk over his head while Madame Seguin showed me my seat. In the confusion caused by this last episode, and by his being carried away by Marie, screaming and spitting with rage, I sat down next to the Russian priest and opposite Mademoiselle Ambatielos. M. Seguin took a loaf of bread from a three-legged basket at his elbow and carved it against his chest. Soup was served—with vermicelli letters of the alphabet floating in it. These were last straws to the little Seguins' table manners.

" Maman, Yvonne's got more letters than me." " Maman, Helène keeps taking my letters out with her spoon." " Children ! Children ! Quiet, quiet ! " said Madame Seguin gently. " No, don't do it." Hélène seized Yvonne's plate and pulled it towards her. " Stop," said M. Seguin, who was like a rat, with spectacles all misted over with soup steam. " Hélène, leave the table. Go to Marie." Exit Hélène, with her apron over her head.

Soup was followed by chestnuts and brussels sprouts. All the time the Russian priest, who wore a pale blue tie with a buttoned frock coat and a moustache fierce as a Gogol novel, kept up a flow of conversation with Mademoiselle Ambatielos. She looked very young. She was stout, with a high firm bust decorated with a spray of artificial roses. She never ceased touching the roses or her blouse or hair, or looking at her hands—with a smile trembling on her mouth and her blue eyes wide and staring. She seemed half intoxicated with her fresh young body.

" I saw you this morning when you didn't see me," said the priest. " You didn't." " I did." " He didn't, did he, Madame ? " Madame Seguin smiled, and carried away the chestnuts, bringing back a dish of pears.

" I hope you will come into the salon after dinner," she said to me. " We always chat a little—we are such a small family party." I smiled, wondering why pears should follow chestnuts.

" I must apologise for baby," she went on. " He is so nervous. But he spends his day in a room at the other end of the appartement to you. You will not be troubled. Only think of it. He passes whole days banging his little head against the floors and walls. The doctors cannot understand it at all." M. Seguin pushed back his chair, said grace. I followed desperately into the salon. " I expect you have been admiring my mats," said Madame Seguin, with more animation than she had hitherto shown. " People always imagine they are the product of my industry. But alas, no ! They are all made by my friend Madame Kummer, who has the pension on the first floor."

Painting Ambrose McEvoy

Two Drawings Derwent Lees

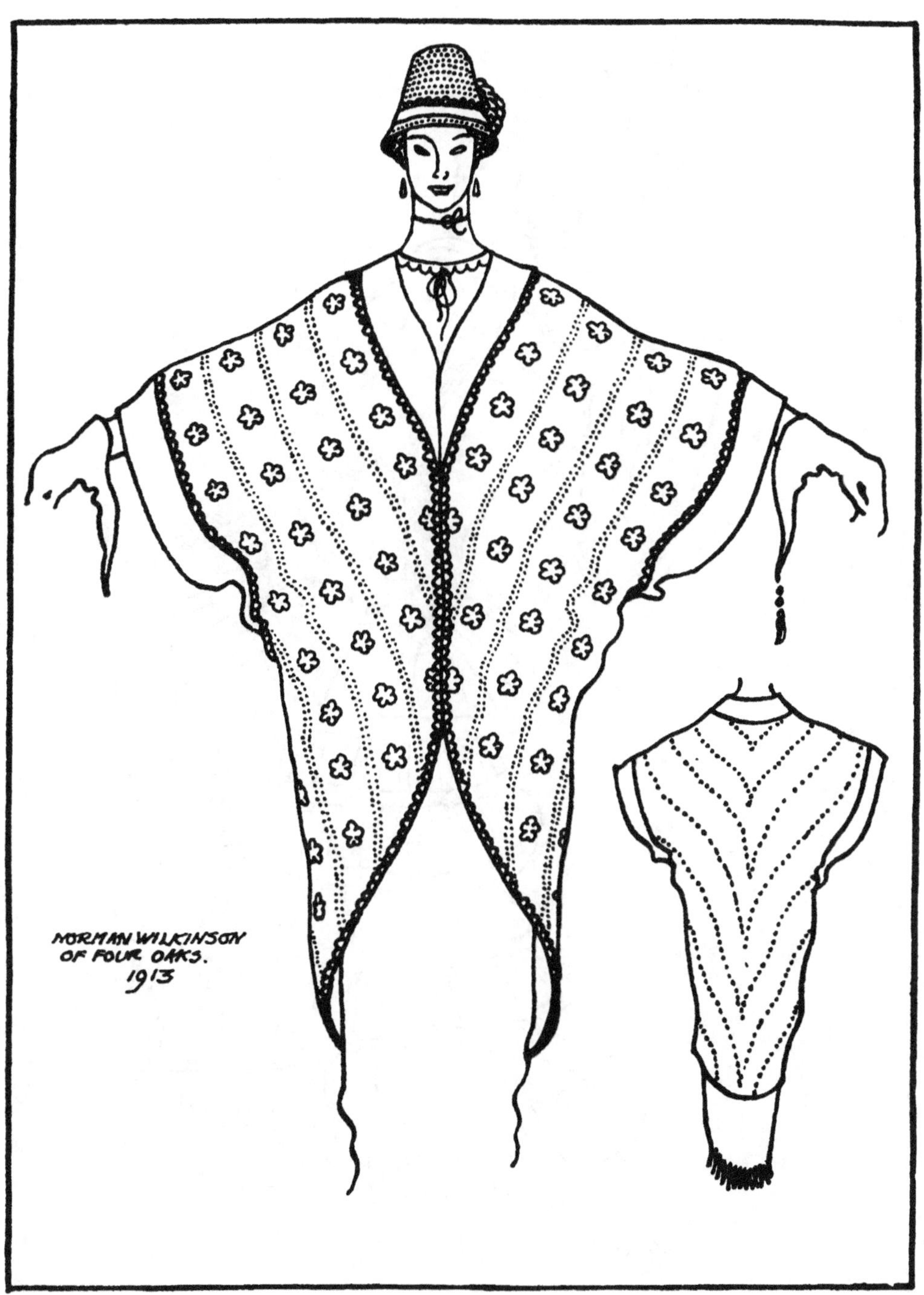

Design for a Wrap   Norman Wilkinson

Design for Fancy Dress Harold Squire

THE THEATRE: By GILBERT CANNAN

Conventions: Chinese, English and French

THERE is at the Duke of York's Theatre an ingenious entertainment called The Yellow Jacket, which purports to be a Chinese play in the Chinese manner. Whether it is really Chinese or not does not matter. It is sufficiently like The Mikado and Willow-pattern and unlike The Letters of John Chinaman to be accepted by an English audience. What is important is that it is an entertainment which does perfectly set up its conventions for the evening's purposes. It has no change of scene. The author of the piece and proprietor of the troupe of actors announces the shifting of the scene—" 'Tis a room in the palace of Wu Sin "—" 'Tis a love-nest," etc.—and, because he believes in the transformation, his words carry conviction. All the machinery of the stage is exposed. There is absolutely no deception, as the conjurer says, and the audience is trusted to deceive itself, and it does so. Unfortunately for it-self this deception does not lead to anything, because the American authors have, like so many of their English colleagues, been concerned more with stage trickery than with any dramatic idea. They have trusted too much to the novelty and the humours of Chinese convention and have failed to see to it that the play itself, which moves through that convention, should be imaginative and charming. In fine, this Chinese play is infected with the vices of the Western theatre to such an extent that its own virtues do not appear and the entertainment does not invariably entertain: indeed, without Mr. Frederick Ross as the Chorus and Mr. Holman Clark as the Property Man there would be very little fun at *that* theatre. The actors, as is so often the case, are left to make the best of a poor business and so it is not from China that we are to look for help, though the magnates of the theatre will no doubt ransack the Far East and the Further West before they begin to look at home for dramatic fare to lay before the English public.

It seems very certain that, the Court Theatre school having

carried their revolution so far, and seeming impotent to bring it to a head, there will be in the main theatres of London a pleasant reaction. It is not without significance that the youngest of the actor-managers should produce the masterpiece of old Sardou, the greatest of theatrical conjurers. " Absolutely no deception, ladies and gentlemen. The quickness of the action deceives the eye." The idol of Francisque Sarcey had a diabolical ingenuity in using the theatre to create in his audience a sort of spurious excitement, very like that of " spotting winners." He lays a scent, crosses it, doubles, trails aniseed across it, brings you to running water, bears you off on a chase after nothing, gives you an evening's occupation that has neither rhyme nor reason, impresses you in your excitement with his marvellous ingenuity and leaves you in cold blood to realise his incurable futility. You are not asked to believe and you do not believe in any of the characters of the play. You are not asked to set up any convention except it be a convention to assume the cleverness of M. Sardou and your own imbecility. Once that is granted then the play proceeds to pick its way through the maze. It is not elevating but it is, up to a point, amusing. Unfortunately the fashion on which that kind of thing lived is dead, for we have gained a certain degree of efficiency in a finer use of the machinery of the theatre. We have made room in the theatre, if not for beauty, at least for an idea or two. Worst of all (for Sardou and Sarcey) we have begun to think our theatre in London superior to the theatre of Paris. We are beginning to want to use our own conventions and to use them to some purpose, or, again, we are inclined to make a convention of the absence of conventions and to say, Be hanged to action, give us character. Mr. Arnold Bennett, for instance, in The Great Adventure, has the most fantastical and flimsy excuse for setting the machinery of the theatre in motion. He has a wildly improbable story which is hardly at all susceptible of exposition in terms of drama, but his interest is centred in his two characters of the painter and Janet Cannot, and by these he justifies himself of the demand he makes on our time and pockets (I always pay for my seat in case I may have in all good faith to insult author and manager). He says with his admirable common sense: " I can entertain you in my own way. I can provide admirable opportunities for actors and actresses." Agreed. All the same, the pleasure that is to be got in the theatre from the revelation of character in dramatic action is keener and, more profitable than that which is to be got from the leisurely and, so to speak, extrinsic exposition of character for its own sake. It is all a matter of convention, and I find that we have, after all, something to learn from the Chinese.

Let me add that we have nothing at all to learn from the Japanese of Melchior Lengyel in Typhoon, which is pure but not very competent Sardou. In spite of all the industry and ingenuity that have gone to the making of the play and its production, no sufficient convention is set up. The action of the play is not affected by the hero's being a Japanese, and the over-elaborate colouring of the Japanese element jars with the thread-bare French textures of the piece. All the labour to induce conviction of something that is fundamentally untrue and clearly irrelevant to the action produces exhaustion and a sort of irritation to which the excitement of the effective theatrical scenes come as such a relief that many people will believe that Typhoon is a tolerable play. It is not nearly so good as Diplomacy.

FICTION By HUGH WALPOLE
A New Book by Charles Marriott

MODERN English criticism, allowing as it does that Poetry and Essay and Drama are fit subjects for its most serious attention, nevertheless denies the novel similar privileges : the modern novel, it gives us to understand, is, when popular, bad, and when unpopular pretentious, and behind this general principle there lurks a conviction that the art of selection is in modern fiction an impossible thing and that, at any rate, even when a selection is made, nobody cares. The endeavour in England to notice every novel that is published must lead to certain disaster, and the fact that the novel about which most people wish to read notices is, as a rule, the novel about which there is the least, critically, to be said, adds to the difficulties. Finally, it is beyond question true that the general level of English fiction is, at the present moment, high, and this very quantity of adequate work adds to the confusion of the critic's duties.

The critic, confronted with novel after novel that would, with its cleverness and ability, have surprised the forties and fifties into amazed applause, has, nevertheless, to admit that the passage of these same volumes through this modern world is swift and inglorious, three months being, on the whole, their allotted span of life. He is then forced to conclude that the standard of the English novel is higher in 1913 than it was in 1850 ; then why, if that be the case, does no novel published to-day seem assured of any immortality ? In short, by what standards is the critic of to-day to arrange his rewards and penalties ?

The first and immediate necessity, if one is to deal in any ordered fashion with the two thousand novels hurled annually at the head of an amiably indulgent public, is the necessity of selection, and this selection must be made in accordance with certain rules, and these rules must come immediately from one's own direct question, What do I personally want from the novel ? It may be taken for granted that what I personally want is in no way the same thing as what Mr. S—— or Mr. M—— require, but, allow them to formulate their rules and proceed to their individual judgments, and compare those judgments with my own, then, at any rate, from the three conditions of selection, some interesting definition may be gathered.

The qualities, then, that I require of the modern novel are a conviction of personality, a knowledge of life and a love of form and, of these, I believe the first to be the most essential. The novelist of to-day is confronted with a thousand examples of his art, whereas the novelist of a hundred years ago had the undiscovered world before him ; again and again, to-day, we are confronted with the most admirable and lifelike imitations of other people's masterpieces and these imitations may, critically, be dismissed at once : a second Fielding, a second Meredith, even a second Arnold Bennett is of less value to us than a first Mary Brown or a genuine James Robinson.

It is, however, one of the most encouraging signs for the believer in the health and strength of the English novel of the twentieth century that so many evidences of this same individuality are to be found ; during the months of the present year we have had Mr. Cannan's " Round the Corner," Mr. Marriott's " Catfish," Mrs. Belloc Lowndes' " Studies in Love and Terror," Miss Meynell's " Lot Barrow," Miss May Sinclair's " Combined Maze," and Mr. Oliver Onion's " Debit Account," and in all of these personality, knowledge of life and sense of form are (in various degrees) to be discovered ; in all these novels there is to be found an intellectual courage and a determined honesty that is beyond all praise.

Although Mr. Cannan may owe something to the greatest of modern English novels, " The Way of All Flesh," Miss Sinclair something to Mr. Hoopdriver and Mr. Lewisham, and Miss Meynell something to Jane Austen, there is evidence of enough individuality here to support the optimists and confound the faint-hearted, but, of them all, Mr. Charles Marriott has in " The

Catfish " (Hurst and Blackett, 6*s*.) produced the outstanding novel of the present year, and it is in " The Catfish " that I find the most complete fulfilment of my three essentials. If at the present time the standard of criticism had been less confused, the author of " The Column," " Genevra," " The Wondrous Wife," and " Now ! " would have been rewarded with acclamation, but a certain almost frigid distinction, a determination to advance no single step towards the coloured appreciations of the public lest any atom of personality should be sacrificed, have hindered his popularity, and the poetry of " Genevra " and " The Wondrous Wife," the sharp brilliance of " Now ! " and " The Kiss of Helen " are still waiting for their sufficient acknowledgment.

Towards this acknowledgment " The Catfish " will surely assist him, for now, for the first time, there is some softening of that earlier coldness and a fine tenderness, unusual in Mr. Marriott's work and, hitherto, the great quality lacking in it, has crept into his pages.

In watching the work of the younger English novelists of to-day one is struck by the fact that they have all of them the same end in view, namely, to represent the most modern aspects of modern life in some form that may be true to both realism and romance. If it be true that " realism is the prose, and romance the poetry, of things seen " (and this is a very halting definition) then this general characteristic is proved to be true. Mr. Onions lights a sordid murder with the colours of flashing sky-signs and wet lamp-lit streets—Mr. Cannan plunges into the heart of his sordid family an adventurer with a soul as romantic as the forests and deserts that he has encountered—Miss Sinclair, as she traces the misadventures of a half-starved little clerk in a garden city, makes of a Polytechnic drill a dance that beats, rhythmically, through every page of her history—Miss Meynell introduces into her tragedy of a servant-girl the figure of a sailor whose passion for the romance of the sea colours the whole history. And so with them all. The younger English novelist is concerned with the romance of the most material of modern phenomena, and that is no mean life-work.

This is, most emphatically, Mr. Marriott's concern, and " The Catfish " is a most eloquent example of it. " Quite early in life George Tracy discovered that if he were to be reasonably happy and prosperous he must pretend." Here in Mr. Marriott's first sentence you have the note of the book.

It is George Tracy's intention to be prosperous, it is also his especial fate that he should be accompanied, to the end of his days, by his imagination. He sees quite clearly (like all Mr. Marriott's heroes his perception is always sharper than that of his companions) that this imagination of his will interfere with this same prosperity unless some especial use be made of it, and during the first half of the book, the reader observes his attempts to discover what his fellow-beings do with their imagination, if they have any, and in what way success is to be helped by imagination without becoming unpractical. How to combine the selling of soap with the delight in the thunders of a waterfall is the book's question, and do we not then instantly perceive that here Mr. Marriott is precisely in line with the other more individual novelists of this generation ?

Tracy notices that modern business can be assisted in its most practical issues by this same element of romance, and finally he establishes a shop that by this very combination of the hard-headed realist and the dreaming idealist secures for every individual customer his heart's desire.

Tracy does not arrive at his solution without help, and in the character of Mary Festing Mr. Marriott has given us a most delicate and elusive character. So elusive is she, as she appears and disappears throughout George's history, coming to his aid, almost against his will, suggesting this and that link in the chain of his discoveries, finally vanishing when he has made his solution, that we, the readers, are not tangibly conscious of her existence. She is the finely coloured figure symbolising this interpenetration of realism and romance for which he is searching. She keeps his soul alive, forbidding the poetry in it to make it loose and casual, forbidding the prose its harder, less visionary qualities. She is, finally, " the Catfish "—" for the catfish is the demon of the deep and keeps things lively."

In its evidence of personality this beautiful book is, of course, abounding. No one living or dead, save Mr. Marriott, could have written it. In its knowledge of life, also, it is surely sufficient. In spite of the poetry of its theme, no single concession is made to the spirit of untruth. Mr. Marriott's shop is a perfectly practical, possible shop: his soap and his hair-brushes are marked with their priced tickets, and their value is the best possible for the money. On the other hand, the imagination of George Tracy is exactly the imagination that a modern man of affairs may be permitted to possess: the waterfall, the garden, and that little vision of Cornwall: " It wasn't so much what might happen as what things *meant*; the sulky way the hills at the back of Porth Enys bumped along to the Land's End; the sudden woods of ash-trees in the valleys; the stealthy turns of the road from Porth Enys to Porthlew, the magic of the Mount in grey weather "—these things are of the very stuff of life.

Finally, in no earlier book of his has Mr. Marriott displayed, so magnificently, his sense of form. His was a theme that tempted to over-writing, over-description, over-emphasis. Never is there a word too many, never is that art of suggestion of which he is so fine an exponent allowed to degenerate into artificiality.

For originality, for reality, for economy this book is, indeed, a book of mark.

GENERAL LITERATURE By FRANK SWINNERTON

The Final Word

IT is a clear sign of the death of the Victorian spirit that so many of our younger critics should now be saying the final word about its various exemplars. Mr. Chesterton, in a brilliant and wonderful book, "The Victorian Age in Literature" (Williams and Norgate, 1s. net) has run off a strangely simplified list of great names, with characteristic *elan*. Another much abused book has recently dealt discouragingly with the literature of the nineties; and an anthology of Victorian verse has shocked both poets and precisians by its daring extension of the Victorian era to our own day. All sorts of monographs upon the Victorian writers, artists, and notabilities are appearing; and it is noticeable that, for the most part, they reveal a resolve that this new Georgian Age should really begin clear of all muddled notions of its amorphous predecessor. Mr. Lascelles Abercrombie, who has already enriched the new age with eloquent poetry, has discovered in Mr. Thomas Hardy the one novelist who has raised his craft to the level of the major arts ("Thomas Hardy: A Critical Study." Secker. 7*s*. 6*d*. net). He has introduced his proposition with a fable, in which man's surplus imagination rather vaguely demands of art the complete expression and exercise of "those inmost desires which in ordinary experience are by no means to be completely expressed." He elaborates the idea of man's need, and appears thereby to have given Art a definition; which, however, is not the case, for the book, by saying what need Art satisfies, completely avoids saying what Art is. It may be questioned, in this connection, whether Art is not a stimulus to man's imagination rather than an employer of waste energy. Mr. Abercrombie has a very vigorous intellect, and his book is distinguished by a sense of form which gives it unique value in Mr. Secker's handsome series. I cannot help regretting, therefore, that his parade of intellectual dignity and philosophic reasoning puts difficulties in the reader's way, and that he should have been tempted into developing a theory of the novel which is appropriate only to Mr. Hardy. It does not seem to me any good to make a theory out of Mr. Hardy's novels simply in order momentarily to rank the novel with the other arts. It is surely the critic's function to inquire into the nature of that which is (I mean, in formulating a general proposition), and not to seek to found an art on a purely arbitrary metaphysical basis. Mr. Abercrombie's present theory, however logical, tends to exalt one man and his method over all other methods whatsoever. Mr. Hardy is a rural novelist. The English novel, on the whole, is urban ; and urban life is more complex, and, in a way, less seizable than country life. Its characteristics are less positive. If our urban novelists are less imposingly rigid in their metaphysic than Mr. Hardy it is not because they are " timid " : it is because their material, being diffused, does not permit truthfully of such simplicity of form as Mr. Hardy's. When an artist is ridden by his metaphysic, so that it becomes a tyrant rather than an interpreter, his art is the less perfect. Mr. Abercrombie, bent upon establishing a declared philosophic basis for Art, is inclined to subdue this fact, because his own sympathy lies in the direction of austere Classical determinism. But he should not write as though the accident of Mr. Hardy's situation was a condition of Art. For most of his particular criticism, I have nothing but admiring appreciation. It seems to make worth while the sheer intellectual effort which at times is necessary in order to understand some of the rather portentous writing. And it should be recognised that the book is by far the best appreciation of Mr. Hardy that has appeared. It is a book which defies the ordinary kind of kick-and-run review, both by its profundity and its highly emphatic pride in unusual possessions.

Mr. Abercrombie has not much to say about the Victorians. He is content to refer to " the spirit of the time." But Mr. Martin Wood (" George du Maurier : The Satirist of the Victorians." Chatto. 7*s*. 6*d*. net) is very pointed and frequent in his allusions, as becomes the biographer of a satirist. To Mr. Wood it seems desirable to describe the Victorian age as one of sentiment, as one without humour and without vulgarity. It was impossible, according to Mr. Wood, for a Victorian to be an artist ; and accordingly the real artists " of the time " sought their inspiration outside The Town and the age. Mr. Wood himself is clearly entitled by many congenial sympathies to write about du Maurier, and the book is very entertaining as well as very inclusive. Du Maurier does not represent a particularly Victorian attitude of amused shrewd tolerance of many things which, in our own age, to the rebuttal of the charge of frivolity, produce more violent emotions. He tolerated sentimentality, because he indulged in it; he laughed at the social ambitions of the newly rich because he neither resented nor feared their intrusion upon himself; he admired the Victorian conception of gentility because it embodied the Victorian hybrid of chivalry and utilitarianism. And, like all the Victorians except Dickens, who was a common man with passionate sympathies, his humour often indulgently displayed itself in polite facetiousness and—especially in his novels—in a sort of tender benignity which is not calculated to survive the Victorian age. All this is illustrated and aptly hit off in Mr. Wood's book, which has large claims upon the public. Mr. Wood has seen du Maurier kindly and microscopically; and he is good at exposition and commentary. His writing is rather like that of dainty old letters, in faint ink, scrupulously small, with what might seem an anxious dread of being commonplace. The outcome, although both generous and enthusiastic, is studiously moderate, and is contained in a long and rather charming series of modest "happy thoughts." At times, when showing his sympathy with du Maurier's preference for joyous, pleasant things, Mr. Wood becomes merely silly, as when he says: "It seems to have been left for modern artists to grow wealthy and live comfortably upon the proceeds of their own relation of the world's despair; if they are playwrights, to live most snugly upon the box-receipts of an entrapped audience unnerved for the struggle of life by their ghastly picture of life's gloom." He becomes on page 121 very Victorian indeed, by proclaiming, by way of emphasis, that "Summer is as great as Winter." But elsewhere he very prettily expresses himself upon a host of other things, and really shows the perception that we should expect from his gentle emphatics.

It is some sort of reflection upon the impermanence of du Maurier's serious art that the illustrations to "Harry Richmond" make the reader uncomfortable. The novel seems in recollection so much richer than these drawings, which belong pathetically to a period of low artistic vitality. It is in reading Mr. R. H. Gretton's "Modern History of the English People" (Grant Richards, two volumes, *7s. 6d.* net each) that we see some explanation of this low vitality. "Harry Richmond" was published in 1871, and, according to Mr. Gretton, it was several years later that a new spirit was infused into Art. At first the newly endowed middle-class was bent only upon "something different," with the result that the Victorian theories—as, for example, in street decoration—were succeeded by a passion for rococo effects. The middle-class "allowed itself to be told that many of its surroundings were ugly, and it substituted for them others of a different taste with exactly the same superficial attention." William Morris "was roused to fury, not by blank impenetrability on the part of the middle-class, but by the quality of its susceptibility," which, in fact, showed no truer idea, but only a fresh misunderstanding. It hastened to become artistic, without any real new vision, like any eager, well-intentioned person who hastens to execute instructions before he has grasped them. So for a time the eighties showed confusion. But they were better than the seventies, because they were actually in turmoil, however mistaken. And in the seventies the particular mid-Victorian flow of energy had dwindled, while the diverse energies of the final quarter of a century were not yet apparent.

It would not be possible to do anything like justice to Mr. Gretton's book in the present chronicle, because it is the history of a busy time, very much compressed, and very intricate. It does not compare with the late Justin McCarthy's "History of Our Own Times," for the reason that it is more comprehensive, more incisive, and more expert. McCarthy was a political journalist who wrote fluently about the things in which he was interested. Mr. Gretton is a critic who, in 450 pages, has described the extraordinary tumult of eighteen years (from 1880 to 1898). When the second, and concluding volume of his book appears, I shall hope to return to it. Meanwhile we may perhaps glance at a sentence from his preface germane to our present subject. Mr. Gretton writes: "The death of Queen Victoria closed an epoch, but the new epoch was to throw light upon that which preceded it." Now it will have been noted that Mr. Gretton's book is to survey the history of England up to the year 1910. It would not be very daring to suggest that by that year the various forces of the Victorian age were either exhausted or so clearly defined as to throw the entire period into relief. The result has been shown in the books published since 1910. We have a tolerably clear series of concurrent activities in the Arts—some of which have grown powerful after long, silent preparation, some of which are due simply to a consciousness of untrammelled youth. With these active movements towards the manifestations of a new contemporary art, there has come the critical activity which leads those at the beginning of a new era to examine the corpses of ancient energies by the light of distinct, unprejudiced intelligence. Criticism of the Victorians has been Victorian : it is now something else. Before now, it has said—in a Victorian phrase—" We are still too near . . ." Now, we can accept Mr. Chesterton's critical nonconformity, and Mr. Abercrombie's philosophistry, and Mr. Wood's quietly mannered epigraphs, in the sanely critical spirit of Mr. Gretton's analysis of forces and tendencies. And the development is all to the good, because the variety in critical standards, no less than the variety in creative methods, is in all probability a proof of new and sanguine vitality.

FRENCH BOOKS By J. MIDDLETON MURRY

THOSE who admire the puissant genius of Balzac will finda certain keen pleasure in reading every page of his strange medley of criticisms (" Honoré de Balzac, Critique Littéraire." Introduction de Louis Lumet. Messein, 7 fr. 50) published in the series of unsuccessful newspapers produced by him between the years 1830 and 1840. The first of these ventures was the *Feuilleton des Journaux Politiques*, in which appeared by far the greater mass of his articles. This was followed by the *Chronique de Paris* (1835), *La Caricature*, and finally, when Balzac was at the height of his fame, by the *Revue Parisienne* (1840), in which appeared his best critical work, including his famous article upon Stendhal's *Chartreuse de Parme*. The cumulative effect upon the reader of this collection of criticisms is in the main one of amazement at Balzac's encyclopaedic interests. There is in this book the same tumultuous desire for universal knowledge that finds its expression, at a higher emotional level, in the *Comedie Humaine*. In the *Feuilleton* we find Balzac reviewing scientific treatises on the Laws of Light, military text-books upon cavalry exercises, and an exposition of the Pauline Epistles ; and in all cases we find his criticism competent and informed by a genuine enthusiasm for universality. But such reviews possess at the best an antiquarian interest for their curiosity's sake. It is well to have them collected. They may always afford an afternoon's enjoyment and an increase of our unceasing wonder that Balzac could have done the countless things he did.

Of far different quality and deserving far different treatment are the essay on the *Chartreuse de Parme*, the article on Sainte-Beuve, and the two criticisms of Hugo's *Hernani*. Balzac disapproved of *Hernani ;* but his critical motives expressed in his first article are of the highest. " Il est donc d'autant plus utile que ce drame soit jugé consciencieusement, que, si l'auteur était dans une fausse voie, beaucoup de gens le suivraient, et que nous y perdrions, nous, des chefs-d'œuvre sans doute, et lui son avenir." These are the reasons why Balzac devoted a detailed and searching criticism to *Hernani*. " We will examine in succession," he wrote, " the conduct of each person, then the *ensemble* of the drama and its aim ; and finally we will inquire if this work marks a step forward in dramatic art ; and, if it does so, in what sense it does so." Probabilities, and above all the intrinsic logic of character, are set at wilful defiance in the play ; and to the character of Charles V. Balzac devotes one of the most significant passages in the book.

" A drama is the expression of a human passion, of an individuality, or of some great deed. *Phedre* is the example of a drama expressing a passion. *Henry IV.*, *Henry V.*, or *Richard III.* are examples of the drama that expresses an individuality. In each work the genius of the poet has originally translated a human life, whether it be Racine who idealises it, or Shakespeare who presents it with every nuance. Schiller in ' William Tell ' represented a deed with its accessories : men, passions, interests. All three arrived at the aim of dramatic art. But here the character of Charles V. does not belong to any of these three theories. Don Carlos does not express events, character, or passion. He might be called Louis XIV. or Louis XV. Perhaps M. Victor Hugo wished to find the formula for Royalty." And Balzac follows out his criticism relentlessly until he reaches the conclusion : " L'auteur nous semble, jusqu'a présent, meilleur prosateur que poète, et plus poète que dramatiste. M. Victor Hugo ne rencontrera jamais un trait de naturel que par hasard ; et à moins de travaux consciencieux, d'une grande docilité aux conseils d'amis sévères, la scène lui est interdite."

Between Balzac and Sainte-Beuve a great gulf was fixed. It may be that in part Balzac's hostility to Sainte-Beuve was due to the treatment that he had himself received from Sainte-Beuve ; but in truth the barrier between them was Jansenism. Balzac often forgot that he was a Roman Catholic, but at heart he always was, and he remembered it when he criticised " Port-Royal." Sainte-Beuve for him is the past-master of *ennui*. " As you read M. Sainte-Beuve, *ennui* soon falls upon you, as you sometimes feel a fine rain fall and finally soak you to the bones. Phrases, with ideas too tenuous to seize, rain down upon you one by one and sadden the intelligence that exposes itself to this humid French." To Balzac, Sainte-Beuve's style is finnicking. " He goes led by an idea to collect a tiny bouquet "—and he returns laden with a bundle of hay. If Balzac could have abated a little of his spleen he would perhaps have said that Sainte-Beuve was exercising a most delicate power of selection ; and would have found in him something akin to the genius he so warmly recognises and champions in his article on *Chartreuse de Parme*.

When we recollect the treatment that Stendhal received during his lifetime, during the whole of which he went practically unrecognised, there appears something magnificent in Balzac's eulogy, " M. Beyle has written a book in which sublimity breaks forth in every chapter. He has produced a work which cannot be appreciated save by men of the highest souls, at a time when it is but rarely that men even *discover* great subjects and then only after having written a score of extremely spiritual books." Doubtless Balzac was vaguely conscious of the presence in Stendhal of a power that he himself never had, a sense of perfect form and balance by which in *Le Rouge et le Noir* and in *Chartreuse de Parme* we are given a picture of society in which manners never predominate over men nor men over manners. Stendhal had a lesser gift than the author of the *Comedie Humaine ;* but his gift was in greater perfection. Balzac did not see this clearly ; but he did recognise clearly and without hesitation that Stendhal was a man of genius. He devoted to the book one of the most masterly pieces of genuine critical analysis that has ever been written ; and championed Stendhal in 1840 when Stendhal himself prophesied that he would but begin to be read in 1880.

" I have read the book for the third time lately ; I have found the book ever more beautiful, and I have felt in my mind the happiness that comes from the prospect of doing good.

" Is it not doing good to endeavour to do justice to a man of immense talent, whose genius will be discerned only by the eyes of some privileged beings ; the transcendence of whose ideas deprives him of that immediate but passing popularity sought by the courtisans of the people and despised by great souls ? If mediocrities knew that they are given a chance of raising themselves to the company of the sublime by understanding them, then *Chartreuse de Parme* would have as many readers as *Clarissa Harlowe* had when it appeared."

L'Ordination, by Julien Benda (Emile-Paul, 3 fr. 50) has been a stumbling block to the Académie des Goncourts. Together with *Les Filles de la Pluie*, by André Savignon, it came before the ten members for the final choice of a Lauréat des Dix. By the casting vote of the President, M. Benda was defeated. The judgment has received a considerable amount of criticism in France ; nor is the attack upon it undeserved. I confess that my acquaintance with M. Savignon's book upon life in Ushant has been confined to a leisurely glance through its pages in a bookshop ; but its faults are so manifest that the acquaintance is sufficient. *Filles de la Pluie* is chaotic, and therefore not a work of art. It is notes and sketches for a book—very good notes and sketches—but yet not a book. Confined to somewhat rhapsodical descriptions of primitive life in a stormy Atlantic island, the book lacks even the first shaping of the creative imagination. By its choice the Académie des Goncourts has weakened its already unsteady reputation.

L'Ordination is, if barely a great book, at least a good and sincere book. Its theme is to be found in a phrase, " La pitié c'est la mort." Felix, the student of philosophy, of whose soul the book is an analysis, has fallen in passionate love with Madeleine, the wife of an unsympathetic commercial husband. Madeleine becomes for a year the mistress of Felix, who finds that his love for her begins to die. Felix realises that Madeleine is wholly in love with him and absolutely dependent upon him, and in the very moment when he decides to break the liaison for ever he begins to pity her. His thought turns to her, broken, abandoned and helpless without him, and from the pity rises something of a new love. Between the new love and his passion for philosophic contemplation follows a terrible struggle. Felix leaves Madeleine for a time, only to return and watch her from a hiding place.

" Elle leva là tête : il vit ces traits d'enfant devenus en huit jours des traits définitifs, où rien ne jouait plus, et où les signes de la souffrance faisait moins mal à voir que ceux de la volonté ; il vit cel œil vitreux, comme vidé de son ressort, où rien ne tendait plus, où rien n'attendait plus. . . . Maintenant elle était au pied de la montée qui ramenait chez elle, et elle montait lentement, comme trainant avec elle toute la quotidiennité de sa lourde existence et toute sa servitude. Et il pensa : ' Elle remontera comme ça tous les soirs de la vie ! ' Alors il n'y tint plus. Il voulait lui crier :

' Madeleine, tu n'es pas seule. . . . Je ne te quitte pas. Je t'aime.' Il voulait sortir de son ombre, courir à elle."

Felix let Madeleine pass without a word. His power of pity was exhausted. " He had in his veins the poison of pity, yet death had not come to him." Thus ends the ordination. Felix marries and has a baby girl, and devotes himself to his passion for philosophy. Ten years later the second part of the book, *La Chute*, begins.

Felix is living with, yet apart from, his wife and child, wholly devoted to abstract thought, gradually becoming more and more remote from them. One day the little girl tires very quickly and falls ill ; and Felix during the night comes to look at her. He vaguely recognises the symptoms of a spinal disease ; and as suspicion becomes certainty, a great wave of pity comes over him breaking down the walls of his intellectual detachment. Henceforward comes the old bitter struggle between the brain and the heart, of the life of the intellect and the life of love ; and after weeks of torment love has the victory.

Of this book it is easy to say that the theme is as old as *Naturam expellas furca : tamen usque redibit*, and that there is nothing more. The essence of *L'Ordination* is the nature of the defeat and the nature of the victory. In the first part the brain has the victory of the heart. Felix will not say the word as he watches Madeleine leave her house. He has put Madeleine from him ; and he is broken. In *La Chute* the heart has the victory of the brain. Felix leaves the life of speculation for his baby girl ; and he is conscious of his own defeat, that he has abandoned the better part, and that the ideal of his true self is lost for ever. It is not a case of expelling Nature with a fork. The moral values of the intellectual and the family life are at least equal. There is no fundamental rightness in the victory of instinct over the intellect ; and the tragedy is that they cannot be reconciled. If you choose so to put the case, *L'Ordination* is the statement in its barest and simplest terms of the problem which the philosophy of M. Bergson glosses over. " Instinct " or " Intuition " is no panacea for the realities of life. The intellect and the desires of the intellect are as potent and as valuable to their possessor as instinct and the blind impulses of instinct. It has not been given to M. Bergson in the twentieth century to solve the difficulties and quiet the groanings of St. Paul.

It is very necessary to appreciate the intense humanity of the theme of " L'Ordination," because its artistic expression has not kept all its unity. I think that no critic who is at the same time a writer of fiction himself could doubt that the first part of the book is a piece of absolute autobiography, written with the intense simplicity and restraint of " a soul that has suffered." It is the directest statement possible of the most terrible mental struggle a man can undergo, when his love for a woman fails and turns to pity. It is a masterpiece of its kind. Not a word rings false. There is no loose-lipped sentimentality, no maudlin regret. Compare it with a book which English criticism has been content to hail as " great," August Strindberg's " Confessions of a Fool," a welter of vicious sentimentality, against which *L'Ordination* stands like a Greek statue against the image of obscene Ashtaroth.

In *La Chute* we are conscious that the directness of personal experience has been lost. Yet even here there are one or two passages describing the very process of the true intellectual life which have an echo of the passion of Plato's Symposium in them.

" Il venait de découvrir la vie intellectuelle—la vraie vie intellectuelle—non plus le caressement des idées qu'il avait connu comme tous ceux de sa classe au sortir du collège, non plus le frôlement des doctrines entre une visite et un dîner, mais l'étreinte passionée, permanente, exclusive, les semaines entières passées à creuser un concept sans penser à autre chose, l'action fiévreuse de ce creusement, et les transes de l'échec, et les joies du triomphe, et la fécondation haletante de l'idée par l'idée, et l'être entier tendu comme d'une tension d'amour pour savoir si telle idée descend de telle autre ou bien si c'est le contraire."

But in spite of such passages the whole effect of the second part as compared with the first is that of an intellectual construction that has lost touch with the intense reality of personal experience. The intellect clarifying the vision and restraining the emotions produced *L'Ordination ;* the intellect alone without an emotional basis produced *La Chute. La Chute* is but a logical extension of *L'Ordination*. M. Benda is a philosopher, and not an artist. He lacks the true creative imagination which might have transfused the reality of the first part into the second. The Académie des Goncourts has committed a twofold error.

It has passed over a book that is almost great for one that is assuredly mediocre. It has moreover committed an error which can never be repaired ; for I am convinced that M. Benda will never write such a book again. *L'Ordination* is not the result of an artist's instinct to create a great story ; but of the wounded man's instinct to tell of his sufferings. And to this tale, without other sufferings, there is no hereafter.

GEORGIAN MUSIC By W. DENIS BROWNE

The Balfour-Gardiner Concerts

THE second series of Balfour Gardiner concerts ought to have convinced the public at last that the young generation of composers must be taken seriously. At the four concerts that have recently been given we have heard a number of orchestral works by a group of writers, who, if they have not at present sufficient cohesion to be called a school, are well on the way to found one in the near future, provided only they have the necessary determination and patience.

It is not at first sight an easy problem to trace the descent of the family of composers that has suddenly appeared in our midst. At the end of the nineteenth century the sole hopes of English music were Stanford, Parry (whose last work, an admirable symphony, was played at the first of these concerts), and Elgar. There had been no musician of note since the days of Sterndale Bennett, except Sullivan, and there was little actual musical life in the country outside the chief national institutions. As a matter of fact, we were at this time prostrate under the crushing weight of the Brahms cult, with its attendant formality and Teutonic heaviness : and it was not until well on in the twentieth century that we were able to free ourselves from the toils of a music which a French critic could only desperately describe as " d'une pudeur d'éléphante qui se déshabille." Having no music of our own, we did obeisance before this god, following him blindly and unreasoningly. It is not to be wondered at that our national stagnation increased instead of diminishing.

The training of a musician at this period included harmony, taught first, and counterpoint, taught second, an order of teaching which had a particular bearing on subsequent developments. A pupil learned naturally to attach more importance to the earlier study than to the second. That is, he learnt from the first to think in chords, or vertically, instead of in melodies, or horizontally ; and this attitude was helped by the comparative decadence of singing and by the ubiquity of the pianoforte. Such a training would render a young musician peculiarly susceptible to the influence of a movement that was soon to make itself felt on the Continent. Debussy and others were experimenting with harmony for its own sake, and writing music which depended for its effect solely on the juxtaposition of unresolved discords. Strauss was working on somewhat similar lines in Germany, Puccini in Italy. It was not surprising that young British composers, tired of Brahms and estranged from counter point, should fall an easy prey to music which was both easier (when you had your models) and more exciting to produce than dry fugues and sonatas. They did indeed fall an easy prey, and some of them, like Cyril Scott, have not yet struggled out of the toils. Others, however, have just escaped, and some of these we have lately been hearing. But the harm that has been done by borrowing French and other foreign methods is very real : it is one of the greatest disasters that has ever happened to music. I mean the blow that has been dealt to counterpoint. If counterpoint and the logical habit of mind that counterpoint implies are taken away from us, the highest potentialities of music will be lost for ever. Among our young composers Percy Grainger can still write counterpoint, and it is for that reason that he is so virile and direct. But his compositions (which have been so far only in the smaller forms) when he gets away from folk-songs, are merely and shockingly sentimental. One very important thing, however, he has done, and that is to show once more that no instrument can equal the human voice in expressiveness when it is allowed to vocalise freely, unhampered by words. The old monks knew it when they introduced wordless *melismata* into plain chant. The Italians knew it in the eighteenth century when they improvised *rifiorituras* during an operatic aria. They knew something else too. They not only made their singers study composition, but they made their composers study singing. It is partly because we have forgotten how to sing that our composers are being led off into harmonic vagaries as artificial as they will eventually be meaningless. As long as they are content to borrow the latest thing in harmony from abroad and to fit it on to English ideas that have no relation to it, counterpoint being cast to the four winds, so long will the balanced judgment of posterity find their works as fruitless and ineffective as we to-day should find a work composed entirely of a succession of diminished sevenths. Harmonic music relied originally on the effect produced by relief following on tension, *i.e.*, a resolution following a discord. Modern harmonic music, however, it has recently been said, is not based on this principle at all, but on the theory that no discord necessarily implies a resolution. This is a stage of development that has not yet really been reached in England, where most of our composers have only got as far as working on a basis of cheating the ear of its expected resolution by a continued series of discords, the tension thus created being artificially prolonged until the composer sees fit, as he generally does, to relax it at the conclusion of the phrase. The fullest development of the theory is to be seen in Busoni and Schönberg, who (this is important) have returned to a way of thinking that is very definitely contrapuntal. The curious result of their experiments is that their harmonies, produced quite secondarily and accidentally through the aid of counterpoint, are infinitely more varied and interesting than the intentional and primarily produced harmonies of the French school. When Percy Grainger, therefore, is contrapuntal, as in " Green Bushes " and " Molly on the Shore," he is clear and forcible and harmonically interesting as well. When, as in " The Inuit," he relies solely on harmonies for his effect, he is no better than a mid-Victorian hymn-writer. A somewhat similar combination of strength and weakness is to be seen in Vaughan Williams. He has a stronger personality and a greater power of continuous musical thought than most of his contemporaries. Instead of doing what the music wants him to do, he makes it do what he wants himself, and the result, though sometimes a little rough, is invariably a definite expression of the thought behind it. In the " Fantasia " on Christmas Carols," when the chorus are singing contrapuntally against the solo voice or each other, the effect is strong enough; it is noticeably weakened when they confine themselves to supplying harmonies to the solo part. A much more vital work by the same composer is his " Variations on a Theme by Thomas Tallis." It is austere in conception and massive in design, and beautiful as well, and it could only have been written by one who fully understands the music of the old masters in its relation to present day needs.

Another composer with a personality and a brain which he knows how to use is Gustav von Holst, who conducted three of his own works at these concerts, a pair of Eastern Pictures for female voices and harp, " The Mystic Trumpeter," and " The Cloud Messenger." His tests (which latterly he has made himself) are based on Eastern writers, and he knows how to fill his settings of them with a colour that though generally low-toned is always interesting and often beautiful. In " The Cloud Messenger," he contrives to maintain throughout a definite atmosphere, quite distinct from mere local colour ; and the way in which he sustains the interest is the more remarkable in view of the lowness of his tones. He never hesitates to prolong a figure or a phrase indefinitely and yet it does not pall. Altogether this was a remarkable work.

Perhaps the least satisfactory production of the whole series was Granville Bantock's " Fifine at the Fair." Gifted with remarkable skill as an orchestrator, he contrives to combine the maximum of instrumental parade with the very minimum of musical thought. Ideas there are in plenty, but they are bad ones. Reduced to their lowest terms, they hardly deserve consideration ; but they are tricked out so brilliantly as to deceive an unthinking audience. After this heavy-handed commentary on Browning it was a relief to listen to Arnold Bax's symphonic poem, " In the Faëry Hills." Though it fails a little in interest at the end, mainly through looseness of harmonic structure, it is an honest and on the whole successful attempt to express abstractions in the language of the orchestra. The call on the horn does not represent, as Bantock would have made it do, the actual notes of the fairy horn ; we hear it, not as a tune but as a symbol. Similarly the little dance theme is not essentially a dancing tune, but it conveys very clearly the idea of a fairy dance. The treatment here can be contrasted with Bantock's fair in " Fifine " ; a jumble of blaring steam organs, old men playing fiddles, and little boys blowing penny whistles. It is cleverly done, but one has only to set beside it Stravinsky's treatment of a similar idea in "Pétrouchka," to see its absurdity.

Several other composers were represented at these concerts, among them Delius and Frederic Austin, the former by a revised version of his " Lebenstanz," and a pleasant early pianoforte concerto. Frederic Austin's Symphony deserves notice, firstly because it was the only large orchestral work performed that had no programme attached to it. This is a relief. Surely it is time we gave up labelling our music in this stupid way. Tiresome and misleading analogies between music and the other arts have led composers to depend for inspiration upon external stimuli, upon which music need not depend any more than logic or mathematics. Secondly, it was interesting because it was a definite attempt to solve in terms of music certain problems of musical thought,and to prove that though the symphony with its conventions about subjects and keys is extinct, yet it may be possible to revive the essential spirit that lies behind it in a less conventionalised form.

This is the second season of these performances. What has been the net gain ? The pond of English music has been considerably stirred up and a deal of life, and some weed, brought to the surface. The really important thing is not so much that the public has been able to hear the works, though public recognition is important, but that all these composers have been able to hear each other. Meanwhile for it all they have to thank one man, who characteristically included only one, and that a very small one, of his own works at the tail end of the last concert.

THE GALLERIES By MICHAEL T. H. SADLER

Anne Estelle Rice

OBSERVANT visitors to the previous exhibitions of Miss Rice's work will notice a very distinct advance in these new pictures alike of skill and enterprise. The contrast is facilitated by the inclusion in the present exhibition of several works belonging to the earlier period—notably Nos. 4, 5, and 33. Miss Rice has mastered her colour. It was apt occasionally either to run away with her, or to remain rather harsh and muddy. It is now her slave. She paints less preponderantly in reds and yellows. She is tackling wooded landscapes, rocks, shadow-covered valleys. Her previous sea pieces were a shimmer of sunlight on golden sand and blue water. Nowadays she paints curling foam over shingle or dark blue water patterned into eddies by the wind. In pictures infinitely more complicated than before, she puts unerring shadows and conquers infinite varieties of plane and distance. And she attempts all this because form to her no longer means principally surface-form, but roundness and substance. She seems to wish to get her hand round to the objects she paints—to express their solidity. This change is not surprising, when one remembers that the structural quality of nature and buildings and human bodies, is the quality which is everywhere attracting the young artists. No. 5, " L'Eventail vert," has already been mentioned as an example of the earlier ideal. Built on a framework of strong, rhythmical lines, the picture is a decorative arrangement in brilliant colouring. It is flat ; not with the symbolistic flatness of Egyptian art, but rather with the flatness of a Japanese colour-print, which is really a compromise between pattern and representation. Then turn to No. 23, " The Market Place," and the difference is plain. Here is even less naturalism, but infinitely more reality. The advance is in colour and form alike. There is no very bright colour in " The Market Place," but yet the picture has the brilliance of southern heat, and glows more than " L'Eventail vert," for all the latter's orange and vermilion.

By the time this criticism appears, innumerable writers will have jumped on the suggestion of Cubism in Nos. 13 and 15. Let us be clear in using this unlucky word. The Cubists seem to me to fall into two groups. There are those who, like Miss Rice, love structure and content, who love a tree as a definite cubic element in a landscape, a human body for the firmness of its cubic anatomy. This group are " realists " because they keep in touch with nature. The other line of Cubism leads away from reality to spiritual expression. Picasso and his imitators follow the inner lead of any natural object, through a maze of angles and balanced lines. They have abandoned representation. Like Kandinsky they are searching for the inner meaning of natural objects. But unlike Kandinsky they work on intelligence and not on feeling. This must be taken, not as a general dogmatic assertion, but as a personal opinion. Kandinsky is to me a musician of colour and line, but the harmony of Cubist music has not touched me.

Returning, however, to the realm of the more or less material, whatever one's opinion of Picasso, it is clear that he and Miss Rice are not on the same tack. It is to be hoped therefore that no one will be led astray by the rather loose talk in the newspapers, which classifies Post-Impressionism, or anything new in art, as Futurism or Cubism. Miss Rice, in so far as she paints trees and hillsides in planes, is cubifying, but her Cubism is a very long way from the solemn inanities of Derain's latest oils or the tentative naughtiness of the Grafton Group. Miss Rice has a sense of humour and does not forget that she is "cubifying" in order to express, and not expressing in order to cubify. The result is that these are fine pictures (No. 15 especially), rich and living. In a slightly different form the same tendency appears in her tree trunks, which Miss Rice is painting under a new convention, and successfully. But I hope she won't allow the practice of setting a patterned tree in the right foreground to become a habit. The English water-colourists did so, Turner did so, even Gauguin did so. An almost identical tree appeared in three or four pictures in this exhibition, but while three or four may delight, there comes a time of satiety.

In the painting of flowers Miss Rice shows real genius. Whether it be an almond-tree in flower or flower pieces pure and simple, the result is splendid. The force and vitality of this painting as a whole is the important thing. Many artists nowadays are vigorous, but not all of them know when vigour stops and fireworks begin. And that knowledge is Miss Rice's treasure of sanity.

REVIEW OF REVIEWS: ENGLISH, FRENCH, ITALIAN

I. The English Reviews

"POETRY and Drama" is a notable newcomer among the quarterly reviews. Though the bulk of the magazine is to be devoted to criticism, a number of pages in each number are to be given up to the publication of new verse. It is not necessarily any disparagement of the prose articles (though some of them have rather an undergraduate swagger about them!) to say that the creative work is more interesting than the critical. Lascelles Abercrombie's verse is always arresting; and his short play "The Adder," which was recently produced at the Liverpool Literary Theatre is, in some respects, the most challenging thing he has done. The editor of "Poetry and Drama" is fortunate in having secured so distinguished a contribution to his first number. Among the prose-articles, perhaps the most interesting are Edward Thomas's mock eulogy of Ella Wheeler Wilcox, and Henry Newbolt's gallant and discriminating appreciation of "Georgian Poetry, 1911-12." Poems by James Elroy Flecker, Maurice Hewlett and Michael Mecredy, and critical papers by Rupert Brooke, Harold Monro, Algar Thorold, A. Romney Green, Leonard Inkster, J. Rodker, Gilbert Cannan, Richard Buxton and F. S. Flint go to make up what must be considered a promising first number.

In "The Manchester Playgoer," John Palmer continues his lively controversy with Gordon Craig; and the number also contains articles by W. L. George, Gilbert Cannan, O. Raymond Drey, Horace Holley and J. H. Mandleberg; a short play by Gwen John, and drawings by J. D. Fergusson.

The April number of "The English Review" opens with a long poem (or rather a series of short poems, loosely strung together) by William H. Davies, on the old theme, Town versus Country. Rather formless as a whole, "The Strange City" contains passages as delightful as anything Davies has done: and the poem has certainly more distinction than the academic elegy on Swinburne, by John Helston, which neighbours it. Two papers on literature, one written from the inside, or artist's, point of view, the other from the outside, or critic's, point of view, would seem to let us into the secret of the business, and tell us how it is done! "The Story-Teller's Craft," by Arnold Bennett, is a neat and dexterous little lesson in the art of seeing things; while, in "Literature as a Fine Art," R. A. Scott-James, having picked up a few hints dropped by the artists themselves, has, after the manner of critics, tried to formulate them as generalisations.

The only contribution to the April "British Review" which possesses any artistic interest is W. B. Yeats's poem, "The Grey Rock"; though we make no pretence of having read through Canon Rawnsley's sequence of sonnets.

To "The Forum," which always devotes a deal of space to verse, Bliss Carman contributes a series of what he calls "Rhythmics," which he introduces with the following suggestive note:

"The poems printed herewith are taken from a number of Studies in Greek and Latin Mythology. They are brief monologues or descriptive poems in lyric measures, intended for recitation to the accompaniment of music and dancing or interpretive motion.

"This novel art, a blend of reading, music and acting, has been gradually evolved in an attempt to find an adequate instrument of training for higher physical education or personal harmonising,—an instrument which enlists ecstasy and intelligence in the play of physical exercise, just as they are always enlisted in desirable life. It is a true art, else it never would have served this comprehensive use. It is simple enough and untheatric enough to be adaptable for home use and for primary education, and yet comprehensive enough to be worthy of the complex and subtle skill of the best dramatic artist. It is more lyric than acting, more ornate than reading, more natural than opera, and effects the transformation of poetry into visible beauty in a unique and compelling way. It maintains and enhances the legitimate sorcery which dwells in poetry, by giving full value to its rhythmic quality, and it renders the instinctive and primal fascination of dance more rational and noble by supplying it with a theme worthy of its technique.

"Poems written for the purpose of such presentation must necessarily conform to certain limitations. They cannot meander at will in the delightful fashion of long meditative lyrics. They must be full of action and movement as an old ballad. Even their similes, metaphors and references, should be translatable into the language of plastic motion or suggestion. They must be lyric in form, yet always somewhat dramatic in feeling and scope."

II. The French Reviews

The *Mercure de France*, in its origin and conception certainly the greatest of all French reviews, has after twenty-three years exhausted the creative impulse which used to animate it. It has not evolved with the evolution of other methods and men ; and its excellences to-day are the same as they were ten years ago : in the first place, the excellence of organisation which makes the *Revue de la Quinzaine* an invaluable record of the world's artistic progress ; in the second the unfailing standard of one or two of its original contributors, chief of whom is Remy de Gourmont, whose fortnightly " Lettres à l'Amazone " are a mine of delicate and contemplative wit. In the most recent number before us as we write (March 16), the original contents are rather dull. The poem by Louis de Cardonnel, " A Figline," is not up to the writer's best level. A rather bizarre short story based upon the psychology of dual personality by Marie M. Bonnet is the best contribution in a somewhat mechanical number.

Le roy est mort : vive le roy ! The April number of *La Nouvelle Revue Française* affords ample evidence that it is around this review that the majority of the genuinely creative French writers of the present day are grouping themselves. It is, however, by no means a young review or even a " new review." André Gide, Emile Verhaeren, the late Charles Louis Philippe, Gabriel Mourey, André Suarès are all mature writers, all nearer fifty then twenty years of age—and perhaps the most striking characteristic of *La Nouvelle Revue Française* is its mature eclecticism. The April number begins with a delightful article by André Gide upon the ten best French novels. André Gide has many English admirers—though we doubt whether Mr. Edmund Gosse's rather uncritical eulogy in his latest book of studies has seriously increased their number—and it will be of considerable interest to them at least to learn M. Gide's selection. We hope to publish a translation of this brief article.

Besides, there are other good things in *La Nouvelle Revue Française*—a further fragment of Ch. Louis Philippe's unfinished story of his childhood, " Charles Blanchard," preceded by an account of Philippe's difficulties in writing it, by M. Léon-Paul

Farque; " Journal d'un Milliardaire," by Valéry Larbaud; and M. André Suarès' " Chronique de Caerdal."

The fact that M. André Gide places Stendhal at the head of all the novelists of the world is in itself a justification, were any needed, of the special number of *La Revue Critique* (March 10) devoted entirely to Stendhal. From unpublished fragments of Stendhal's Journal to a careful study of Stendhal's finances by M. Adolphe Paupe, and a delightful article upon his clothes by M. Eugène Marsan, the number is a mine of Stendhaliana, invaluable to every admirer of the great novelist. We intend to refer to this number at greater length. The last number before us (March 25) is naturally something of an anticlimax. It contains, however, an interesting article for lovers of literary antiquities, by Charles Le Goffic, " Le Ménage de Jean Racine," and its usual complement of excellently critical reviews.

L'Art Decoratif (March) continues its admirable series of critical articles upon recent painters, with an article by Mlle. Lucie Cousturier upon Henri-Edmond Cross, who died in May 1910, at the age of fifty-four. Cross was a Neo-Impressionist whose work is not generally as well known in England as that of Seurat or Signac. Nowadays we find the spotty technique of the Pointillists rather tiresome and *demode*, and this technique still comes between us and a genuine appreciation of the undoubted merits of Cross. At the end of his life Cross himself was working away from it, as may be seen in his latest water-colours. But if we accept Pointillism, balancing its excellences against its deficiencies, it must be acknowledged that Cross's work provides some of the finest examples of that technique, particularly in " Les Petites Montagnes Mauresques " which is beautifully reproduced in colour. The other articles include " L'Art Nouveau sur le Paquebot France "—which does not seem any better than any other " new art "—and a charming account of " Coiffures et Bonnets anciens " by Raymond Crussard.

Note. Le Temps Present (March): A delightful and characteristic " Leçon Poétique," by Francis Jammes; " Poème," by the Comtesse de Noailles; and an erudite article upon " Les Lais de Marie de France " by Mlle. Henriette Charasson.

La Phalange (March 20: Three " Soirs de Flandre " by

Emile Verhaeren; "La Renaissance Lyrique actuelle et la Tradition," by Henri Hertz.

L'Ile Sonnante is an excellent number, containing a scene of "Diane de Poitiers," by Maurice de Faramond; "Le Chien Empoisonné," a sketch by Louis Pergaud; and good poetry by André Salmon, Fernand Divoire, Tristan Derème, Paul Vimereu.

III. The Italian Reviews

In *La Voce* (March 27) is an article of great interest, "Il teatro musicale dell' ironia e lo stile dello Strauss," by Gianotto Bastianelli, in which the writer argues that Strauss, morbid in his choice of libretto, is in the conception and execution of his work essentially decadent. With great artists, their conception of action is identical with their religious conception of life. Their nature has two aspects, that of the hero and that of the saint. The world of passions cannot be revealed to the artist in its full value unless the artist himself sees a value in them; unless he discovers, in the light of a faith that transcends the material naturalness of the events, a profound significance in them. The dilettanti of religious belief and of passino, like D'Annunzio, Wilde, Hoffmannsthal lack this sense of value. First, they cannot judge the passions, and their effort to do so turns in upon itself and produces a sad and almost unconscious irony. To such writers Strauss is the musical counterpart. But Strauss does differ from them, in that he has the courage to recognise this ironical attitude in himself, and to emphasise it by a greater honesty of style. The rottenness of the school of D'Annunzio consists in pretending that underneath the pomp of a grandiose style there exist faith and passion which are not really there. The ironist in literature should have the courage of his irony. This is what Strauss has done. He has found a style that is adequate to the monstrosity of the decadent drama, and he has found it automatically, unconsciously, almost by "motor reaction."

"The ferociously parodistic, chaotically Rabelaisian style of Strauss gives the decadent drama its perfect form without any equivocation between the truth of the action and the preciousness and idealism of the language. . . . The irony of Strauss is expressed directly and indirectly. To its direct expression belong his rhythm, the colour of his instrumentation and his harmony, his counterpoint, etc., which in Strauss are full of never-ending violence and surprises. To its indirect expression belong all the *double-entendre*, the musical insinuations and suggestions, such as taking up stylistic specimens of other composers, and the adoption of a number of methods discovered by his predecessors or contemporaries—adoptions which in the humorous context of Strauss's compositions (and sometimes even where it does not appear to be humorous) always convey a sense of parody." M. Bastianelli gives as examples the parody of Meyerbeer in "Also Sprach Zarathustra."

An examination of every one of Strauss's works reveals an almost unvarying irony of the composer's mind towards his own statements, which, expressed by means of a formula almost always derived, imitated and parodied, produce upon the audience the impression that the composer did not only disbelieve in it, but laughed at it with violent ironical scepticism. This irony is not Socratic, believing and seeking, but the "very decadence and degeneration of irony." "The decadent theatre," concludes M. Bastianelli, "cannot be saved except by the strident laughter of a fierce and gigantic irony. Strauss, unlike all the insincere modern poets, has been able to do this spontaneously, by a simple instinct to save himself at least in part. And should we hesitate to honour the ingenuity of music that is not so corrupt as its poetry, and to give praise to one who is certainly our greatest modern musician in spite of the fact that like others he degrades both faith and passion?"

The *Rassegna Contemporanea* (March 10), which now appears fortnightly, contains a short story by Matilde Serao, "Beata," not particularly different from a number of other competent stories which she has written in the past. The psychological conflict is in this case between a young lady and her father, an aristocratic man about town who has left his family. There is also an informative article upon a Balkan writer—Ivo Vojnovich of Ragusa—whose dramas, completely unknown in England, have made him the chief literary hero of the Pan-Slav movement.

Volume I Number II JUNE 1913 One Shilling Net

THE BLUE REVIEW

LITERATURE DRAMA ART MUSIC

MARTIN SECKER PUBLISHER
NUMBER FIVE JOHN STREET ADELPHI

The Imprint

May 17th, 1913

A BRIEF SKETCH OF THE HISTORY OF WOOD-ENGRAVING: By J. H. MASON
POST-IMPRESSIONISM: By A. S. HARTRICK, A.R.W.S.
LITHOGRAPHY: IV. DRAWING MATERIALS: By F. ERNEST JACKSON
TRIFLING WITH THE CODE: By JOSEPH THORP
SOME 18TH CENTURY SONG BOOKS: By WILLIAM MAAS
PRINTER'S LIEN: By C. D. MEDLEY
DECORATION & ITS USES: V. By EDWARD JOHNSTON
TEN HONEST MEN: II. By A MASTER PRINTER
INTAGLIO PRINTING: By DANIEL T. POWELL
THE PLAIN DEALER: V. By EVERARD MEYNELL
PRINTERS' DEVICES: By the Rev. T. F. DIBDIN: PART V
NOTES AND CORRESPONDENCE. PATENTS

Price One Shilling net

Offices: 11 Henrietta Street, Covent Garden, W.C.
Annual Subscription: 12s. post free.

JUNE

CONTENTS

		Page
Joachim Among the Sheepcotes	By S. Spencer	*Frontispiece*
Yasmin	By James Elroy Flecker	77
The End of the Lonely King	By Norman Boothroyd	78
Lines Spoken at the Opening of the Birmingham Repertory Theatre	By John Drinkwater	79
Millie	By Katherine Mansfield	82
Anger and Dismay	By J. D. Beresford	88
A Fresh Start in Music	By E. J. Dent	97
Epilogue: II.	By Katherine Mansfield	103

CHRONICLES OF THE MONTH

The Theatre:		
Caps, Bells and Legs	By Gilbert Cannan	110
Theatres in the Air	By John Drinkwater	113
Poetry	By Lascelles Abercrombie	117
The Novels	By Hugh Walpole	123
General Literature	By Frank Swinnerton	128
French Books:		
A Classical Revival	By John Middleton Murry	134
Recent French Novels	By X. Marcel Boulestin	138
Music	By W. Denis Browne	141
The Galleries:		
Mr. Max Beerbohm's Exhibition	By Edward Marsh	143
Indépendants and the Cubist Muddle	By O. Raymond Drey	146
Drawings by G. S. Lightfoot, J. D. Innes and Frances Jennings		

Editor: John Middleton Murry
Associate Editor: Katherine Mansfield
Editorial Office: 57 Chancery Lane, W.C.
Telephone 2132 Holborn

Joachim Among the Sheepcotes By S. Spencer

YASMIN

A Ghazel

How splendid in the morning glows the lily : with what grace he throws
His supplication to the rose : do roses nod the head, Yasmin ?

But when the silver dove descends I find the little flower of friends
Whose very name that sweetly ends I say when I have said—Yasmin.

The morning light is clear and cold : I dare not in that light behold
A whiter light, a deeper gold, a glory too far shed, Yasmin.

But when the deep red eye of day is level with the lone highway,
And some to Mecca turn to pray, and I toward thy bed, Yasmin,

Or when the wind beneath the moon is drifting like a soul aswoon,
And harping planets talk love's tune with milky wings outspread, Yasmin,

Shower down thy love, O burning bright ! For one night or the other night
Will come the Gardener in white ; and gathered flowers are dead, Yasmin.

JAMES ELROY FLECKER

THE END OF THE LONELY KING

They brought him down from Kharmadin
Beyond the narrow mountain pass
  That leads again to Murias—
All pale, and worn, and deadly thin,
And covered with sweet-scented grass,
  Upon a lordly palanquin.

They set him on the silver bed—
(The silver bed that seemed so small
  Among the pillars of the Hall).
No sound was heard : no word was said,
As secretly they worked the pall
  With shining moons of silken thread.

The hours dragged heavy in their flight,
Yet none paid heed unto the King ;
  There seemed no air of sorrowing
As in the feeble candle-light
They toiled at their embroidering
  With eager hands throughout the night.

They shed no tear : they prayed no prayer,
Nor gave the King a benison ;
  But when at last the pall was done,
They covered him with heedless air
All silently ; then, one by one,
  Crept out, and left him lying there . . .

NORMAN BOOTHROYD

LINES SPOKEN AT THE OPENING OF THE BIRMINGHAM REPERTORY THEATRE, FEBRUARY 15th, 1913.

To you good ease, and grace to love us well :
To us good ease, and grace some tale to tell
Worthy your love. We stand with one consent
To plead anew a holy argument—
For art is holy. We, to whom there falls
The charge that men may see within these walls
The comely chronicle of comely plays,
You, who shall quicken us with blame or praise,
Desire alike but this, that here shall spring
Such issue of our labour as may bring
Fresh laurels to the altars that have known
Service of men whose passion might atone
For worlds than this more faithless, men whose names
Are very life—aye, swift and urgent flames
Of living are they. These are over us
To lighten all our travel : Aeschylus,
Euripides, the Sophoclean song,
And Aristophanes who captured wrong
In nets of laughter, lords of the Attic stage,
The fourfold Greek dominion ; and the age
Of nameless poets when the hope began
To quicken from the blood of *Everyman*
Into the splendour of Marlowe's kingly lust
Of kingly life, the glory that thieves nor rust
Can ever spoil, whose name is manifold—
Ford, Massinger, Dekker, Webster aureoled
With light of hell made holy, Middleton,
Chapman, Beaumont and Fletcher, aye, and one
Whom even these the lords of beauty's passion
Might crown for beauty's high imperial fashion
In classic calm of intellectual rule,
Ben Jonson. Sirs, I am nor wit nor fool
To speak in praise of him whose name is praise,

Whose word is on the forehead of the days,
Shakespeare, our master tried and proved how well,
Mortality's immortal chronicle.

Under the warrant of these men we sail,
And theirs whose later labour these might hail,
Congreve and Otway : the Good-Natured Man,
Proud tattered Oliver : Dick Sheridan,
Who played at passion but free-born of wit
Put scandal out to school and laughed at it ;
These few that stand between the golden age
When poets made a marvel of the stage
And—do we dare to dream it ?—an age that stirred
But yesterday, whereof the dawning word,—
Spoken when Ibsen spake, and here re-set
To many tunes on lips untutored yet
For speech Olympian, albeit pure of will,—
Shall ripen into witness that we still
Are countrymen of those glad poets dead ;
The seed is sown, the barren days are sped.

And they who sowed, are sowing ? He, beguiled
By who shall say what envious madness, Wilde,
Misfortune's moth and laughter's new wing-feather,
Remembering now no black despiteful weather :
Hankin, and he, the cleanser of our day,
Whose art is both a Preface and a Play,
And he who pities, as poets have pitied, life
Of *Justice* reft, so driven and torn in *Strife*,
And one who cries in *Waste* some news of man,
And one who finds in the bruised hearts of *Nan*
And *Pompey* tragic and old yet timeless things :
And that dead Playboy, and his peer who sings
Yet of Cuchulain by the western sea—

Opening of the Birmingham Repertory Theatre

Of these is sown the seed that yet shall be
A heavy-waggoned harvest, masters mine,
Gathered by men whom now the immoderate wine
Of song is making ready.

In these walls
Look not for that light trickery that falls
To death at birth, wrought piecemeal at the will
Of apes who seek to ply their mimic skill :
Here shall the player work as work he may,
Yet shall he work in service of the play.
Nor shall you here find pitiful release
From life's large pressure, nay, but new increase
Of life made urgent by these master-men
Who are our captains. Life, and life again—
Tragic or brave, free-witted, gentle, signed
Of beauty's passion or the adventurous mind,
Or light as orchard blossom, motley wear
But life's wear always—that shall be our care
And all shall surely follow. What may be
Hereafter—to the heavens, to us to see
No will transgressing on the poet's wish,
To you to judge the meat before the dish.
May you that watch and we that serve so grow
In wisdom as adventuring we go
That some unwavering light from us may shine.
We have the challenge of the mighty line—
God grant us grace to give the countersign.

JOHN DRINKWATER

MILLIE

By KATHERINE MANSFIELD

MILLIE stood leaning against the verandah until the men were out of sight. When they were far down the road Willie Cox turned round on his horse and waved. But she didn't wave back. She nodded her head a little and made a grimace. Not a bad young fellow, Willie Cox, but a bit too free and easy for her taste. Oh, my word ! it was hot. Enough to fry your hair ! Millie put her handkerchief over her head and shaded her eyes with her hand. In the distance along the dusty road she could see the horses—like brown spots dancing up and down, and when she looked away from them and over the burnt paddocks she could see them still—just before her eyes, jumping like mosquitoes. It was half-past two in the afternoon. The sun hung in the faded blue sky like a burning mirror, and away beyond the paddocks the blue mountains quivered and leapt like sea. Sid wouldn't be back until half-past ten. He had ridden over to the township with four of the boys to help hunt down the young fellow who'd murdered Mr. Williamson. Such a dreadful thing ! And Mrs. Williamson left all alone with all those kids. Funny ! she couldn't think of Mr. Williamson being dead ! He was such a one for a joke. Always having a lark. Willie Cox said they found him in the barn, shot bang through the head, and the young English " johnny " who'd been on the station learning farming—disappeared. Funny ! she wouldn't think of anyone shooting Mr. Williamson, and him so popular and all. My word ! when they caught that young man ! Well—you couldn't be sorry for a young fellow like that. As Sid said, if he wasn't strung up where would they all be ? A man like that doesn't stop at one go. There was blood all over the barn. And Willie Cox said he was that knocked out he picked a cigarette up out of the blood and smoked it. My word ! he must have been half dotty.

Millie went back into the kitchen. She put some ashes on the stove and sprinkled them with water. Languidly, the sweat pouring down her face, and dropping off her nose and chin, she cleared away the dinner, and going into the bedroom, stared at herself in the fly-specked mirror, and wiped her face and neck with a towel. She didn't know what was the matter with herself that afternoon. She could have had a good cry—just for nothing—and then change her blouse and have a good cup of tea. Yes, she felt like that ! She flopped down on the side of the bed and stared at the coloured print on the wall opposite, " Garden Party at Windsor Castle." In the foreground emerald lawns planted with immense oak trees, and in their grateful shade, a muddle of ladies and gentlemen and parasols and little tables. The background was filled with the towers of Windsor Castle, flying three Union Jacks, and in the middle of the picture the old Queen, like a tea cosy with a head on top of it. " I wonder if it really looked like that." Millie stared at the flowery ladies, who simpered back at her. " I wouldn't care for that sort of thing. Too much side. What with the Queen an' one thing an' another." Over the packing case dressing-table there was a large photograph of her and Sid, taken on their wedding day. Nice picture that—if you *do* like. She was sitting down in a basket chair, in her cream cashmere and satin ribbons, and Sid, standing with one hand on her shoulder, looking at her bouquet. And behind them there were some fern trees, and a waterfall, and Mount Cook in the distance, covered with snow. She had almost forgotten her wedding day ; time did pass so, and if you hadn't any one to talk things over with, they soon dropped out of your mind. " I wunner why we never had no kids . . ." She shrugged her shoulders—gave it up. " Well, *I've* never missed them. I wouldn't be surprised if Sid had, though. He's softer than me."

And then she sat, quiet, thinking of nothing at all, her red swollen hands rolled in her apron, her feet stuck out in front of her, her little head with the thick screw of dark hair, drooped on her chest. " Tick-tick " went the kitchen clock, the ashes clinked in the grate, and the venetian blind knocked against the kitchen window. Quite suddenly Millie felt frightened. A queer trembling started inside her—in her stomach—and then spread all over to her knees and hands. " There's somebody about." She tiptoed to the door and peered into the kitchen. Nobody there ; the verandah doors were closed, the blinds were down, and in the dusky light the white face of the clock shone, and the furniture seemed to bulge and breathe . . . and listen, too. The clock—the ashes—and the venetian—and then again—something else—like steps in the back yard. " Go an' see what it is, Milly Evans." She darted to the back door, opened it, and at the same moment some one ducked behind the wood pile. " Who's that," she cried, in a loud, bold voice. " Come out o' that. I seen yer. I know where you are. I got my gun. Come out from behind of that wood stack." She was not frightened any more. She was furiously angry. Her heart banged like a drum. " I'll teach you to play tricks with a woman," she yelled, and she took a gun from the kitchen corner, and dashed down the verandah steps, across the glaring yard to the other side of the wood stack. A young man lay there, on his stomach, one arm across his face. " Get up ! You're shamming ! " Still holding the gun she kicked him in the shoulders. He gave no sign. " Oh, my God, I believe he's dead." She knelt down, seized hold of him, and turned him over on his back. He rolled like a sack. She crouched back on her haunches, staring, her lips and nostrils fluttered with horror.

He was not much more than a boy, with fair hair, and a growth of fair down on his lips and chin. His eyes were open, rolled up, showing the whites, and his face was patched with dust caked with sweat. He wore a cotton shirt and trousers with sandshoes on his feet. One of the trousers stuck to his leg with a patch of dark blood. " I *can't*," said Millie, and then, " You've got to." She bent over and felt his heart. " Wait a minute," she stammered, " wait a minute," and she ran into the house for brandy and a pail of water. " What are you going to do, Millie Evans ? Oh, I don't know. I never seen anyone in a dead faint before." She knelt down, put her arm under the boy's head and poured some brandy between his lips. It spilled down both sides of his mouth. She dipped a corner of her apron in the water and wiped his face, and his hair and his throat, with fingers that trembled. Under the dust and sweat his face gleamed, white as her apron, and thin, and puckered in little lines. A strange dreadful feeling gripped Millie Evans' bosom—some seed that had never flourished there, unfolded, and struck deep roots and burst into painful leaf. " Are yer coming round ? Feeling all right again ? " The boy breathed sharply, half choked, his eyelids quivered, and he moved his head from side to side. " You're better," said Millie, smoothing his hair. " Feeling fine now again, ain't you ? " The pain in her bosom half suffocated her. " It's no good you crying, Millie Evans. You got to keep your head." Quite suddenly he sat up and leaned against the wood pile, away from her, staring on the ground. " There now ! " cried Millie Evans, in a strange, shaking voice. The boy turned and looked at her, still not speaking, but his eyes were so full of pain and terror that she had to shut her teeth and clench her hand to stop from crying. After a long pause he said in the little voice of a child talking in his sleep, " I'm hungry." His lips quivered. She scrambled to her feet and stood over him. " You come right into the house and have a set down meal," she said. " Can you walk ? " " Yes,' he whispered, and swaying he followed her across the glaring yard to the verandah. At the bottom step he paused, looking at her again. " I'm not coming in," he said. He sat on the verandah step in the little pool of shade that lay round the house. Millie watched him. " When did yer last 'ave anythink to eat ? " He shook his head. She cut a chunk off the greasy corned beef and a round of bread plastered with butter ; but when she brought it he was standing up, glancing round him, and paid no attention to the plate of food. " When are they coming back ? " he stammered.

At that moment she knew. She stood, holding the plate, staring. He was Harrison. He was the English johnny who'd killed Mr. Williamson. " I know who you are," she said, very slowly, " yer can't fox me. That's who you are. I must have been blind in me two eyes not to 'ave known from the first.'' He made a movement with his hands as though that was all nothing. " When are they coming back ? " And she meant to say, " Any minute. They're on their way now." Instead she said to the dreadful, frightened face, " Not till 'arf past ten." He sat down, leaning against one of the verandah poles. His face broke up into little quivers. He shut his eyes and tears streamed down his cheeks. " Nothing but a kid. An' all them fellows after 'im. 'E don't stand any more of a chance than a kid would." " Try a bit of beef," said Millie. " It's the food you want. Somethink to steady your stomach." She moved across the verandah and sat down beside him, the plate on her knees. " 'Ere—try a bit." She broke the bread and butter into little pieces, and she thought, " They won't ketch 'im. Not if I can 'elp it. Men is all beasts. I don' care wot 'e's done, or wot 'e 'asn't done. See 'im through, Millie Evans. 'E's nothink but a sick kid."

. . . . . .

Millie lay on her back, her eyes wide open, listening. Sid turned over, hunched the quilt round his shoulders, muttered " Good night, ole girl." She heard Willie Cox and the other chap drop their clothes on to the kitchen floor, and then their voices, and Willie Cox saying, " Lie down, Gumboil. Lie down, yer little devil," to his dog. The house dropped quiet. She lay and listened. Little pulses tapped in her body, listening, too. It was hot. She was frightened to move because of Sid. " 'E must get off. 'E must. I don' care anythink about justice an' all the rot they've bin spouting to-night," she thought, savagely. " 'Ow are yer to know what anythink's like till yer *do* know. It's all rot." She strained to the silence. He ought to be moving. . . . Before there was a sound from outside Willie Cox's Gumboil got up and padded sharply across the kitchen floor and sniffed at the back door. Terror started up in Millie. " What's that dog doing ? Uh ! What a fool that young fellow is with a dog 'anging about. Why don't 'e lie down an' sleep." The dog stopped, but she knew it was listening. Suddenly, with a sound that made her cry out in horror the dog started barking and rushing to and fro. "What's that? What's up?" Sid flung out of bed. "It ain't nothink. It's only Gumboil. Sid, Sid." She clutched his arm, but he shook her off. "My Christ, there's somethink up. My God." Sid flung into his trousers. Willie Cox opened the back door. Gumboil in a fury darted out into the yard, round the corner of the house. "Sid, there's some one in the paddock," roared the other chap. "What's it—what's that?" Sid dashed out on to the front verandah. "Here, Millie, take the lantin. Willie, some skunk's got 'old of one of the 'orses." The three men bolted out of the house and at the same moment Millie saw Harrison dash across the paddock on Sid's horse and down the road. "Millie, bring that blasted lantin." She ran in her bare feet, her nightdress flicking her legs. They were after him in a flash. And at the sight of Harrison in the distance, and the three men hot after, a strange mad joy smothered everything else. She rushed into the road—she laughed and shrieked and danced in the dust, jigging the lantern. "A—ah! Arter 'im, Sid! A—a—a—h! ketch 'im, Willie. Go it! Go it! A—ah, Sid! Shoot 'im down. Shoot 'im!"

ANGER AND DISMAY

A Footnote on the Writings of H. G. Wells   By J. D. Beresford

MR. WILLIAM WATSON believes in Dickens but not in the future of the novel; he has credited the former and discredited the latter quite explicitly in that new collection of his " The Muse in Exile." Dickens is presented as a fighter, and the nature of his belligerency is formulated in the couplet: " He did not fight to rend the world apart, He fought to make it one in mind and heart." I suppose the same thing might be said—by himself, at least—of any propagandist whose temperament was too mild to face the alternative of the sword. We see the magnificent excuse of the Church " militant," that description which was once so perfectly justified, but has no application to the incredibly padded gloves of the modern ring. The truth is that Mr. Watson's statement is absurd, a mere sentimental trifling with ideas. If I fight my enemy I have one of two objects in view; either I desire to silence any further expression of his for ever, or I desire to convince him that I am the better man and that he had better not contradict me in future. I am not fool enough to suppose, however, that my thrashing of him will make him one with me in mind and heart. I know perfectly well that his object was the same as mine, and that if I had been beaten, I might have knuckled under, but I should not have adopted his accursed heresy in the secret places of my mind.

The whole fallacy arises from the sentimentalisation of the word " fight." Dickens was no fighter himself, and he could not portray the fighter. His ideal was the sweet-tempered, flabby propagandist, whose weapon was the model of his own virtuous life. Dickens's only notion of a hypocrite was of one who covered a secret vice by a profession of virtue and humility. When he attempted to draw a real fighter, he always assumed that the person was mad.

Let us descend, for a moment, to a consideration of that maligned and temperamental woman, Mr. F.'s aunt. I confess with joy that I share her contempt for the precocious, do-my-little-best spirit of Clennam. I, too, hate a fool, and envy that wonderful old lady's honesty in openly proclaiming the fact to the fool himself. I have often wondered whether Dickens had not once been confronted by the original of Mr. F.'s aunt; pelted, perhaps—I sincerely hope so—with hard and well-aimed crusts of toast. I can imagine how he would have resented the bold expression and the militant act; he who was so entirely incapable of running amuck. Virtue, not aggression, was his specific, and his ideal of virtue was mid-Victorian; tainted with Samuelism. Was he not, after all, a Smiles of genius? It is an amazing thought that all the great mid-Victorian figures in poetry and fiction were born during that extraordinary period of revolt which lasted from 1780 to 1830, and that they lived through the wonderful year of 1848 without learning a single lesson. . . .

Is it that we may perceive here some formulation of the law of reaction, of the great and increasing beat of the pendulum with its long swing from century to century? . . .

Whatever the cosmic rule which shall account for the alternation, I turn with relief to the contemplation of the real fighting spirit. I was born to witness the opening movement of the diastole: and I have been so far affected by the impetus of my own times that no philosophic reflection will allay the irritation I feel when I consider the ideal of placid acceptance, of resignation, of plenitudinous satisfaction. It all appears so stagnant, so circumscribed; involuted in fold after fold of snug complacency.

Nevertheless in my youth my revolutionary spirit found little material to work upon. I was the son of middle-aged parents; I was hedged about by the old conventions, and I had not the wit or the originality to find a ladder or to tear a hole in the fence. The escalade, indeed, was not rapid when it came at last. My ladder had many rungs, and—to come after so long an introduction to the particulars of my present purpose—I willingly acknowledge that more than one rung was made negotiable for me by the writings of Mr. H. G. Wells.

The first of his books which nudged my attention was " The Wheels of Chance." From one point of view, it has little bearing on the subject of this paper. It is touched by the Smiles tradition. Hoopdriver's potentialities are those of the old disciple ; the best we can expect from him is application to study, he is an indeterminate dreamer with no capacity for iconoclasm. The same thing may be said of his expansion, Arthur Kipps. Both are studies of that undeveloped man who once appeared to their creator as himself—himself at sixteen or so. We find a little passion in these two quite lovable little men, but it is only a weak explosion of hesitating temper.

With " The Invisible Man," however, we have a clear sight of the true Berserker. Griffin comes before us a complete antithesis to the Kipps type—the union is a later development. Griffin is a selfish anarchist. Wrapped in that cloak of invisibility which was to serve him, he hoped, so much better than the wolf-shape of the Norse legends, he is bent on self-aggrandisement. As he develops, the lust of killing grows upon him, he is one against humanity and he dies fighting the world, his hands clenched, his eyes wide open, and his expression one of " anger and dismay." And always as I read that last wonderful account of his career, I forgive him for his obsession with self, for his pig-headedness and his ultimate futility. The form of him returns to visibility in my imagination as it returned to the sight of that little foolish crowd about him, glowing with those two fundamental emotions, " anger and dismay,"—the very elements of man's revolt against imprisonment in the flesh. These are transcendental things ; and they are for me in this connection the basis of study. I take them naked and titanic as two essentials of the artist ; while I admit —not without a faint regret—that they are not the only essentials, and that they represent but two aspects, however well marked, in my image of Mr. Wells—who, by the way, is quite unknown to me except from his works. . . .

With the invisible man, megalomaniac that he was, anger took precedence, and only defeat and death could bring dismay. But when the Berserker is transformed from beast to artist, it is dismay which represents the generating emotion, and it seems to me that it is of a type which is possible only to those who have the power of withdrawal from their surroundings. This elemental dismay of which I speak now, for instance, is of a type quite other to that felt by the sentimental Charles Dickens. His preoccupation with injustice of the Squeers pattern, had the peculiarly human quality which comes from intimacy with the world of men. He battered—a little feebly perhaps—at the heart of humanity, but always he kissed the gods' feet.

Mr. Wells has had the power to stand aside from these preoccupations, and I quote a passage from " The War of the Worlds," which has always appeared to me as certainly representative of phases of his own experience. " At times," he writes, " I suffer from the strangest sense of detachment from myself and the world about me ; I seem to watch it all from the outside, from somewhere inconceivably remote, out of time, out of space, out of the stress and tragedy of it all."

The penalty imposed for the ecstasies of this abstraction, is a return to dismay, and thence to anger—partly, maybe, at the cursed spite which has saddled him with the recognition. The world of those far imaginings is such a fine place, that the immediate presentation of the world as it appears, strikes the dreamer as a fierce impossible horror. He sees all too clearly that he is imprisoned, and if he were of the primitive Berserker type he would end in red rage, amuck among the unspeakable futilities of our present life. But the artist is confined by the necessities of his temperament, he is conscious before all of the urge to create rather than to destroy. In brief moments of madness he may flap his hands wildly and cry out, " Oh ! let us *do* something, for Heaven's sake, do *something* to alter all this " ; but presently the old command will compel him once more, and he will settle down with little spurts of passion and impatience, either to create a picture of the thing he desires, or to display his own vision of the repulsive thing which the mass of mankind accepts as the best of all possible worlds.

It is these spurts of passion and impatience, symptoms of the transcendental dismay and anger of the spirit, that have evoked this tentative analysis. I find them mirrored in the persons of Mr. Wells's stories: in Lewisham's attack upon the sheep-faced Parkson; in Graham, the sleeper, when he is in the "Silent Rooms"; in the time-traveller when "he raved to and fro, screaming and crying upon God and Fate"; in Bedford (another Berserker) blindly killing the Selemites; in Capes smashing glass in his preparation room; in George Ponderevo and Remington, though somewhat more restrained; in other characters too numerous to instance; and finally with a growing difference in Trafford. I have picked out my examples haphazard as they have occurred to me, but I believe that there is hardly a novel or a romance by Mr. Wells in which the signs of this primitive anger cannot be discerned, while I cannot recall (to mark my early antithesis) a single true instance of the same passion in all the novels of Dickens—the nearest approach to it is in the portrait of Mr. F.'s aunt. . . .

I am laying stress on this contrast not because I wish in any way to belittle the genius of Dickens—for whose work I have a great admiration—but because I wish to thrust a particular distinction into prominence. It may seem that I have indicated the distinction as that between the fighting and the merely propagandist spirit, but the thing goes deeper than this. As I see it, indeed, it is a difference between two fundamental attitudes of mind, between the spirits of acceptance and rejection, between worshipping, idealising the past and glorying in the possibilities of the future.

Mr. Wells, if my induction is a true one, has little or no respect for the past. His war is not against individuals but against conventions. He comes out of the transcendental, a bright unprejudiced spirit aghast at the dull prejudices of our civilisation. He sees our futility, our indolence of mind, our blind leaning upon tradition, and it may be that his first impulse was to explain in a few clear sentences the mistakes under which we are labouring, to make one definite statement so incredibly convincing that the world would at once recognise its stupidity.

That impulse, indeed, is the primitive urge of genius. The remedy proposed is of less importance than the great desire to reconstruct. It was in this that Nietzsche was magnificent ; while his disciples (including Strindberg) have failed, in as far as they have adopted only the critical premises and neglected the constructive deduction.

But neither Mr. Wells nor any other prophet, however inspired, can build until he has persuaded mankind to clear the site, and in the present case I see a life work devoted to that magnificent task. His methods may be divided broadly into two categories : a criticism of the present building and an exhibition of the new elevations.

The first category must be subdivided. Under one head falls all that is merely analysis of existing conditions, all that critical attack which admits the stereotyped response, " Have you anything better to offer ? " Under the other with which alone I propose to deal, our civilisation is shown by romantic means to be ephemeral. The assault is shifted from the convention to the individual. The endeavour represents the attempt to persuade complacent, bigoted, unthinking man that his civilisation is impermanent, to lift him momentarily from his contemplation of his surroundings and give him wider vision.

Many of Mr. Wells's romances fulfil this purpose. As I think of that list of books, I remember first how they gave me the delight of living in a changed world, and secondly how they led me to understand that all life, as I knew it, was open to criticism; that it was a phase in evolution, and not, as I had once believed, essential, ordained and static. Those books (I may instance more particularly the " Food of the Gods," " The War of the Worlds," " The First Men in the Moon," " The War in the Air," and certain shorter stories, lifted me from my contemplation of my immediate surroundings. While I read I gloried in the freedom of moving in new worlds. This uplifting was due to my author's gift of presentation, and if the effect produced had been no other than this, I must have written down these romances as a failure. If, for instance, Mr. Wells's romances had been of the same quality as those of Jules Verne—to whom he has been so foolishly and purblindly compared—I should have come back to earth unaltered. I should have had the new experience of exploring air or water in an unknown machine, but I should have had no new sight of the world from the outside.

In the case of the five books I have mentioned, the effect upon myself was permanent. I had been led to look down upon the whole machinery of civilisation from outside. My habit of thought with regard to life was broken. If I did not believe in the possibility of, say, such a discovery as Herakleophorbia IV., I did very truly believe henceforward in the essential instability of society.

(It may be remarked that I have omitted "The Time Machine," and "The Sleeper Awakes" from my list. I have done so because these two books vary quite definitely in intention and method. They do not break but develop; they are in no real sense constructive. "The Sea Lady," "The Island of Dr. Moreau," and "The Wonderful Visit," I have omitted for other reasons. They are more nearly allegories of the older type, and while I do not fail to perceive the essential allegory of "The Food of the Gods," the constructive intention of that work places it in the other category. If Mr. Wells had written only the first five romances mentioned in this interpolation, he might with some slight show of reasonableness have been likened to Jules Verne.)

I see that I have laid myself open to a charge of egotism in thus laying stress upon the effect which these books have had upon my own mind. But I have adopted the first person deliberately because I have found that the majority of readers have read Mr. Wells's romances as they might have read those of the ordinary author ; and so have come back to earth unchanged. And when I consider this amazing blindness and engrossment in personal affairs, I suffer a reflex of that primitive dismay and anger. I desire fiercely to expound and am brought back to that realisation which led me to this long parenthetical explanation, and examination of categories.

For we are confronted with the extraordinary difficulty of opening men's eyes. I have touched briefly on the method of the first category, and the second I must dismiss briefly. This exhibition of the new plans is to be found in such books as " The Days of the Comet," and " A Modern Utopia," but it appears to me that men will not seriously regard the new until they have become dissatisfied with the old, and that they turn from these pictures of a brighter future with the comment, " Very pretty, no doubt, but we have to live in the world as it is."

I see that this imaginary remark directly contradicts the spirit of that earlier reply I put into the mouth of mankind, namely, " Have you anything better to offer ? " but the contradiction is not mine. In my opinion mankind as a whole is as I have thus drawn it. I find both remarks perfectly characteristic of the same type. Both arise from a failure to look out, from the elementary inability to withdraw momentarily from the immediate pressure of life. . . .

So I return—perhaps by a personal example—to a defence of that " anger and dismay " with which I began. I have heard these fine passions criticised, and I am up in arms to exalt them. I am willing to beg the question that they are effects and not causes, but I find that that assumption in no way weakens my championship. For I know nothing of prime causes, and I believe that admission is implicit in all that I have written here, as I believe also that the unthinking adoption of a cut and dried cosmogeny is responsible for much of the blindness which Mr. Wells has so valiantly attempted to cure.

All that I have so feebly and curtly attempted to champion is the militant spirit that lies behind all that has been expressed by these various books, combining so many methods, of Mr. Wells. To me the purpose of them is not many but one. I am conscious of man triumphant in thought, battering not altogether vainly at the feet of the gods. I see man regarding the limitations of the flesh with anger and dismay.

A FRESH START IN MUSIC By EDWARD J. DENT

MUSIC is in the melting-pot, we are told nowadays. Was there ever a time when this could not be said? The great upheavals associated with the names of Monteverdi or Wagner may be perhaps considered to have been exceptional; twenty years ago, say both revolutionaries and reactionaries, there was peace and tranquillity, steady progress and obedience to sound tradition. Yet a reference to Dr. W. H. Hadow's "Studies in Modern Music" (second series, 1895) will show us that in those days it was necessary to make an elaborate *apologia* for the audacities and originalities of Dvorak, a composer who appears now to be remembered only by an occasional amateur performance of his chamber-music. If we are conscious of a state of flux at this moment, the cause is to be sought elsewhere. The real change that has taken place in the last twenty years is the enormous development of musical intelligence in this country. The general public is more interested in music; it is even beginning to be interested in its young English composers. This interest has to some extent raised the standard of their work. Twenty years ago the young English composer was an obedient and industrious lad who thought it the highest of compliments when his teacher in a moment of cordiality said that his work quite suggested Parry or Stanford; and far away in the distant heavens shone the star Brahms, whom all were told to worship, though none could ever hope to imitate him. The young composer of to-day seems much more determined to be himself and himself only: if he is told that his works have a flavour of Vaughan Williams or Delins he feels quite rightly that that is not what he is aiming at, however deeply he may admire either musician. His teachers are consequently beginning to find out that the old methods of teaching composition will not last much longer, and the problem of finding new methods is an extremely difficult one.

Teachers of composition tend to fall into two groups, which we may call the academics and the modernists. The results of their instruction may be observed at any concert where our young composers' works are performed. If we except the few who show a really strong individuality of their own, the crowd of the second-rate either goes on writing well-constructed sonatas and symphonies of the Brahms period and even earlier, or it gives us symphonic poems and " fantasies " which sound very modern at first, but which after a few years time, if not sooner, are seen to consist merely of a string of journalistic *clichés* borrowed from the foreign composers in vogue at the moment.

It is the teachers of the second class who constitute the real danger to our national music. The work of the second-rate academic is so dull that there is no risk of its having any influence on the public, and the first-rate pupil of an " academic " school is probably the better, if he is a real genius, for the careful training. As long as pupils are taught to *think logically in terms of music*, they are safe, and to grasp even the externals of academic sonata-form requires a certain amount of musical reasoning. The modernist does not teach his pupils to think in sounds. Sonata-form, he says, is obsolete, and he may very well be quite right on this point. But has he any constructive principle to put in the place of it ? If one can judge by such results as come to a hearing, he apparently has not. The general rule given to the young composer seems to be that he must let the shape of his work be determined merely by the story chosen for illustration, and that logic may take care of itself, as long as the orchestration is effective, that is, as long as the orchestral effects sound sufficiently like those which have been made familiar to the writers by Strauss, Debussy or Stravinsky.

The tendency of the age, we are told, is towards orchestral music. Pure line, say the modern critics, has had its day, and the future is to express itself mainly in terms of colour. For the further elaboration of this thesis the word " Post-Impressionism " will be found very useful. Having no knowledge whatever of the art of painting, I must apologise for being compelled to restrict myself to the technicalities of music. Helmholtz adopted the word *Klangfarbe*—tone-colour—as a German equivalent of *timbre*—quality of tone; but I see no reason to suppose that the function of "tone-colour" in music is therefore identical with that of colour in painting. The survival of the word *chromatic* is proof that musicians of an earlier age had completely different views on the question.

We must not be misled by false analogies and picturesque phrases. When critics tell us that modern music depends mainly on colour, they simply mean that they themselves are satisfied with music that presents certain varieties of quality of tone, obtained either by combinations of orchestral instruments, or possibly even by combinations of notes sounded simultaneously on one instrument. The rapid complication of the mechanical resources by which music is made audible has in fact dazzled many people so completely as to make them forget the absence of that logical sense of continuity of thought which is the only foundation of true music.

This tyranny of the instrument forms the subject of an interesting paper by Ferruccio Busoni in a recent number of the German weekly, *Marz*. The article bears the title *Neuer Anfang*, "a fresh start." If a young composer writes as he feels, his teacher will be sure to tell him that he does not know how to write for the instruments. "Look at the scores of Wagner or Strauss," he will say, "and learn from them how to score effectively." The result, says Busoni, is that every modern orchestral work presents us with the same complex of sounds—the violoncellos always trembling with exuberance of emotion, the horns making the most of their natural hesitance of attack, the hautboys always breathless and embarrassed, the clarinets always ostentatious of their voluble facility. There is no room for originality of thought, it is crowded out by the necessity of conforming to the conventional modern technique. Beethoven, almost alone among modern composers, ignored the requirements of the instruments, and made them play what he wished. Poor old Beethoven ! say the teachers of composition ; he was deaf and had no idea of orchestration.

"The born creator of the future," continues Busoni, "will first of all have to face the responsibility of setting himself free from all that he has learnt at school, all that he has heard at concerts, all that is reputed to be " musical " ; and when he has cleared his mind of all that is unnecessary, he will have to bring himself into a state of ascetic and devout concentration, which will enable him to listen to the secret voice within him, and ultimately to arrive at the further stage of communicating this message to mankind."

All this is perhaps less revolutionary than it appears at first sight. We are to give up considering the technique of instruments, and simply write abstract music, indifferent to the means employed for translating the signs into sounds. Beethoven's posthumous quartets, I imagine, show some sort of attempt to work on the lines indicated. But the Giotto of the musical renaissance, as Busoni calls him, will have to be a very much greater man than even Beethoven, and we may be pretty certain that his contemporaries will have a proportionately greater difficulty in understanding him. In the meanwhile, what can we ordinary mortals do towards turning Busoni's advice to some sort of account ? It is useless to set about finding a Giotto, but we can at least try to prepare the way for him. The main thing is that we should concentrate our attention on thinking musically, or grasping the principles of musical logic. We must learn to insist on truth and sincerity in the works which are put before us, we must learn to refuse all that is merely formal and traditional, all that dreary waste of artificial art which charitable critics describe as " very musical "—the sad equivalent of what in literature is classed as " scholarly verse." This does not mean that we must burn all our classics, still less that we should throw in our lot with the party of programme-music. It is the writers of programme-music, more than any others, who have fallen victims to the tyranny of the instruments. Let us learn all we can from the classics, let us love them if we will, but let us beware of reverencing them. Moreover, if we are going to study the classics, let us study them widely (not confining our attention solely to Bach, Beethoven and Brahms), and study them always with a critical eye, never accepting any work as great merely because it bears the name of a great man.

In the case of composers, a good case may be made out for a more restricted investigation of the music of the past. Verdi advised his pupils to take no notice whatever of modern music. They were to work hard at fugue-writing, probably in a rather severe style, and to study no classics apparently, except Palestrina and Marcello, the latter as being the best possible model for the declamation of the Italian language. The selection of these two composers (the English reader may substitute Byrd and Purcell if he likes) shows us that Verdi realised the same essential point which underlies Busoni's counsels of apparent anarchy. We can perfectly well afford to make a bonfire of all our instruments, for the best of all instruments will still be left to us—the human voice.

Even if we keep our instruments, it is undoubtedly on singing that all musical education must be based, whether for the ordinary amateur or for the Beethoven of the future. No one can enter fully into the understanding of music unless he can feel every musical idea from the point of view of the man who first conceived it and used his voice to express it. The experience of controlling our lungs and vocal cords is the best possible training, if rightly planned, for the perception of the rhythmical continuity of sound which is the basis of music. Voices have their limitations, we are told ; but have we considered what we might have achieved had we from the days of Jubal devoted as much physical labour to singing as we have done to playing instruments, and as much intellectual energy as has gone to the development of speech ? All instrumental music, except in so far as it is derived from the primitive tom-tom, is originally an imitation of singing, and it is barely two hundred years since the artistic supremacy of the voice began to be contested. It is the last hundred years that has brought about the disastrous virtuosity of the orchestra, the perfection of instrumental mechanism which has made the instruments less human and personal in their expression in proportion as they have become more elaborate in their technique. The primitive hautboy, for instance, was the nearest approach that its maker could contrive towards an imitation of the human voice ; the modern hautboy claims a separate individuality, and has stultified its improvement in fluency and in accuracy of intonation by an exaggeration of its characteristic deficiencies. Music has to be written for it which will draw attention to its being a hautboy and not any other instrument, and in this way the situation has gradually arisen that it is the over-development of mechanical facilities which is blocking the composer's way to real originality. For the present, it is probably in the sphere of chamber-music that we may hope for some attempt to make real progress. The stringed instruments are less tyrannical, they approach more nearly to the ideal of a normal type of musical sound which can be utilised (as Beethoven showed) for almost any idea which the composer wishes to express. The string quartet is almost the only form of music that has had an absolutely continuous history for two hundred years. Debussy and Ravel have found it as satisfactory a medium as Scarlatti for the expression of pure musical thought. It is often said that modern conditions are not favourable to its development ; but the fact remains that the most modern composers, even if they employ the form but rarely, do at least continue to make use of it, and that section of the public which is seriously interested in music continues, though in small numbers, to listen to them. Until we have recovered the use of our own voices, it seems that it is from writers of quartets that we may most reasonably expect new departures—departures that are really new, and that will lead along a road from which there need be no turning back.

EPILOGUE: II. By KATHERINE MANSFIELD

" I met a young virgin
Who sadly did moan . . ."

THERE is a very unctuous and irritating English proverb to the effect that " Every cloud has a silver lining." What comfort can it be to one steeped to the eyebrows in clouds to ponder over their linings, and what an unpleasant picture-postcard seal it sets upon one's tragedy —turning it into a little ha'penny monstrosity with a moon in the left-hand corner like a vainglorious threepenny bit! Nevertheless, like most unctuous and irritating things, it is true. The lining woke me after my first night at the *Pension Seguin* and showed me over the feather bolster a room as bright with sunlight, as if every golden-haired baby in Heaven were pelting the earth with buttercup posies. " What a charming fancy ! " I thought. " How much prettier than the proverb. It sounds like a day in the country with Katherine Tynan.' . . . And I saw a little picture of myself and Katherine Tynan being handed glasses of milk by a red-faced woman with an immensely fat apron, while we discussed the direct truth of proverbs as opposed to the fallacy of playful babies. But in such a case imaginary I was ranged on the side of the proverbs. " There's a lot of sound sense in 'em," said that coarse being. " I admire the way they put their collective foot down upon the female attempt to embroider everything. ' The pitcher goes to the well till it breaks.' *Also gut.* Not even a loophole for a set of verses to a broken pitcher. No possible chance of the well being one of those symbolic founts to which all hearts in the forms of pitchers are carried. The only proverb I disapprove of," went on this impossible creature, pulling a spring onion from the garden bed and chewing on it, " is the one about a bird in the hand. I naturally prefer birds in bushes." " But," said Katherine Tynan, tender and brooding, as she lifted a little green fly from her milk glass. " But if you were Saint Francis, the bird would not *mind* being in your hand. It would *prefer* the white nest of your fingers to any bush." . . . I jumped out of bed and ran over to the window and opened it wide and leaned out. Down below in the avenue a wind shook and swung the trees ; the scent of leaves was on the lifting air. The houses lining the avenue were small and white. Charming, chaste looking little houses, showing glimpses of lace and knots of ribbon, for all the world like country children in a row, about to play " Nuts and May." I began to imagine an adorable little creature named Yvette who lived in one and all of these houses. . . . She spends her morning in a white lace boudoir cap, worked with daisies, sipping chocolate from a *Sèvres* cup with one hand, while a faithful attendant polishes the little pink nails of the other. She spends the afternoon in her tiny white and gold boudoir, curled up, a Persian kitten on her lap, while her ardent, beautiful lover leans over the back of the sofa, kissing and kissing again that thrice fascinating dimple on her left shoulder. . . . when one of the balcony windows opened, and a stout servant swaggered out with her arms full of rugs and carpet strips. With a gesture expressing fury and disgust she flung them over the railing, disappeared, reappeared again with a long-handled cane broom and fell upon the wretched rugs and carpets. Bang ! Whack ! Whack ! Bang ! Their feeble, pitiful jigging inflamed her to ever greater effort. Clouds of dust flew up round her, and when one little rug escaped and flopped down to the avenue below, like a fish, she leaned over the balcony, shaking her fist and the broom at it.

Lured by the noise, an old gentleman came to a window opposite and cast an eye of approval upon the industrious girl and yawned in the face of the lovely day. There was an air of detachment and deliberation about the way he carefully felt over the muscles of his arms and legs, pressed his throat, coughed, and shot a jet of spittle out of the window. Nobody seemed more surprised at this last feat than he. He seemed to regard it as a small triumph in its way, buttoning his immense stomach into a white piqué waistcoat with every appearance of satisfaction. Away flew my charming Yvette in a black and white check dress, an alpaca apron, and a market basket over her arm.

Epilogue : II.

I dressed, ate a roll and drank some tepid coffee, feeling very sobered. I thought how true it was that the world was a delightful place if it were not for the people, and how more than true it was that people were not worth troubling about, and that wise men should set their affections upon nothing smaller than cities, heavenly or otherwise, and countrysides, which are always heavenly. With these reflections, both pious and smug, I put on my hat, groped my way along the dark passage and ran down the five flights of stairs into the Rue St. Leger. There was a garden on the opposite side of the street, through which one walked to the University and the more pretentious avenues fronting the Place du Théâtre. Although autumn was well advanced, not a leaf had fallen from the trees, the little shrubs and bushes were touched with pink and crimson, and against the blue sky the trees stood sheathed in gold. On stone benches nursemaids in white cloaks and stiff white caps chattered and wagged their heads like a company of cockatoos, and, up and down, in the sun, some genteel babies bowled hoops with a delicate air. What peculiar pleasure it is to wander through a strange city and amuse oneself as a child does, playing a solitary game.

" Pardon, Madame, mais voulez-vous " . . . and then the voice faltered and cried my name as though I had been given up for lost times without number ; as though I had been drowned in foreign seas, and burnt in American hotel fires, and buried in a hundred lonely graves. " What on *earth* are you doing here ? " Before me, not a day changed, not a hairpin altered, stood Violet Burton. I was flattered beyond measure at this enthusiasm, and pressed her cold, strong hand, and said " Extraordinary ! "

" But what are you *here* for ? "

" . . . nerves."

" Oh, impossible, I really can't believe that."

" It is perfectly true," I said, my enthusiasm waning. There is nothing more annoying to a woman than to be suspected of nerves of iron.

" Well, you certainly don't *look* it," said she, scrutinising me with that direct English frankness that makes one feel as though sitting in the glare of a window at breakfast-time.

" What are *you* here for," I said, smiling graciously to soften the glare. At that she turned and looked across the lawns, and fidgetted with her umbrella like a provincial actress about to make a confession. " I "—in a quiet affected voice—" I came here to forget. . . . But," facing me again, and smiling energetically, " don't let's talk about that. Not yet. I can't explain. Not until I know you all over again." Very solemnly—" not until I am sure you are to be trusted."

" Oh, don't trust me, Violet," I cried. " I'm not to be trusted. I wouldn't if I were you." She frowned and stared.

" What a terrible thing to say. You can't be in earnest."

" Yes, I am. There's nothing I adore talking about so much as another person's secret. " To my surprise, she came to my side and put her arm through mine.

" Thank you," she said, gratefully. " I think it's awfully good of you to take me into your confidence like that. Awfully. And even if it were true . . . but no, it can't be true, otherwise you wouldn't have told me. I mean it can't be psychologically true of the same nature to be frank and dishonourable at the same time. Can it ? But then . . . I don't know. I suppose it is possible. Don't you find that the Russian novelists have made an upheaval of all your conclusions ? " We walked, *bras dessus bras dessous*, down the sunny path.

" Let's sit down," said Violet. " There's a fountain quite near this bench. I often come here. You can hear it all the time." The faint noise of the water sounded like a half-forgotten tune, half sly, half laughing.

" Isn't it wonderful," breathed Violet. " Like weeping in the night."

" Oh Violet," said I, terrified at this turn. " Wonderful things don't weep in the night. They sleep like tops and ' know nothing more till again it is day.' "

Epilogue : II.

She put her arm over the back of the bench and crossed her legs. " Why do you persist in denying your emotions ? Why are you ashamed of them ? " she demanded.

" I'm not. But I keep them tucked away, and only produce them very occasionally, like special little pots of jam, when the people whom I love come to tea."

" There you are again ! Emotions and jam ! Now, I'm absolutely different. I live on mine. Sometimes I wish I didn't—but then again I would rather suffer through them—suffer intensely, I mean ; go down into the depths with them, for the sake of that wonderful upward swing on to the pinnacles of happiness." She edged nearer to me.

" I wish I could think where I get my nature from," she said. " Father and Mother are absolutely different. I mean—they're quite normal—quite commonplace." I shook my head and raised my eyebrows. " But it is no use fighting it. It has beaten me. Absolutely—once and for all." A pause, inadequately filled by the sly, laughing water. " Now," said Violet, impressively, " you know what I meant when I said I came here to forget."

" But I assure you I don't, Violet. How can you expect me to be so subtle ? I quite understand that you don't wish to tell me until you know me better. Quite ! "

She opened her eyes and her mouth.

" I *have* told you ! I mean—not straight out. Not in so many words. But then—how could I ? But when I told you of my emotional nature, and that I had been in the depths and swept up to the pinnacles . . . surely, surely you realised that I was telling you, symbolically. What else can you have thought ? "

No young girl ever performs such gymnastic feats by herself. Yet in my experience I had always imagined that the depths followed the pinnacles. I ventured to suggest so.

" They do," said Violet gloomily. " You see them, if you look, before and after."

" Like the people in Shelley's skylark," said I.

Violet looked vague, and I repented. But I did not know how to sympathise, and I had no idea of the relative sizes.

" It was in the summer," said Violet. " I had been most frightfully depressed. I don't know what it was. For one thing I felt as though I could not make up my mind to anything. I felt so terribly useless—that I had no place in the scheme of things—and worst of all, nobody who understood me. . . . It may have been what I was reading at the time . . . but I don't think . . . not entirely. Still one never knows. Does one ? And then I met . . . Mr. Farr, at a dance——"

" Oh, call him by his Christian name, Violet. You can't go on telling me about Mr. Farr and you . . . on the heights."

" Why on earth not ? Very well—I met—Arthur. I think I must have been mad that evening. For one thing there had been a bother about going. Mother didn't want me to, because she said there wouldn't be anybody to see me home. And I was frightfully keen. I must have had a presentiment, I think. Do you believe in presentiments. . . . I don't know, we can't be certain, can we ? Anyhow, I went. And *he* was there." She turned a deep scarlet and bit her lip. Oh, I really began to like Violet Burton—to like her very much indeed.

" Go on," I said.

" We danced together seven times and we talked the whole time. The music was very slow—we talked of everything. You know . . . about books and theatres and all that sort of thing at first, and then—about our souls."

" . . . . What ? "

" I said—our souls. He understood me *absolutely*. And after the seventh dance . . . No, I must tell you the first thing he ever said to me. He said, ' Do you believe in Pan ? ' Quite quietly. Just like that. And then he said, " I knew you did." Wasn't that extra-or-din-ary ! After the seventh dance we sat out on the landing. And . . . shall I go on ? "

" Yes, go on."

Epilogue : II.

" He said, ' I think I must be mad. I want to kiss you—and—I let him."

" Do go on."

" I simply can't tell you what I felt like. Fancy ! I'd never kissed out of the family before. I mean—of course—never a man. And then he said : ' I must tell you—I am engaged.' "

" Well ? "

" What else is there ? Of course I simply rushed upstairs and tumbled everything over in the dressing-room and found my coat and went home. And next morning I made Mother let me come here. I thought," said Violet, " I thought I would have died of shame."

" Is that all ? " I cried. " You can't mean to say that's all ? "

" What else could there be ? What on earth did you expect. How extraordinary you are—staring at me like that."

And in the long pause I heard again the little fountain, half sly, half laughing—at me, I thought, not at Violet.

CHRONICLES OF THE MONTH

THE THEATRE

By GILBERT CANNAN

Caps, Bells and Legs

IT is extraordinary how scattered are the impressions to be got in the theatres of London—a good piece of acting here, a colour there, a witticism or two in another place, a tune in another. When you disentangle them you will find always that each moment of pleasure came by accident and existed entirely apart from the general intention. There is a comedy at the Little Theatre by a new and rather skilful writer, a Mr. Vansittart, who dons the cap and bells and jingles them for a couple of hours, during which and to their accompaniment, a comic drama ought to have started, reached its climax, and come to a close. But, though there was a company of very competent actors on the stage, nothing was heard but the accompaniment, so that I was constantly reminded of an undergraduate neighbour I once had who evolved an unvarying accompaniment of C, E and G in waltz time for every tune that happened to stick in his unmusical memory. Impossible when he played, to distinguish anything but his thudding accompaniment. . . It may be said that, as a critic, I have no business when witnessing a play to go back over the years to undergraduate memories. In the theatre, drama can hold my attention (and, I believe, everybody else's) and I can think of nothing else when it is presented on the stage. When it is absent, my faculties are not engaged, and any wandering idea can creep into my head. (That this happens to other critics is shown by the *comptes rendus* in the newspapers.) That Mr. Vansittart's cap and bells played the old C, E and G refrain is regrettable, but, having tested my power to respond to drama with *Hamlet* at Drury Lane, I refuse to believe that the fault was more mine than the author's. I wish him well, and pass on to record other disappointments.

The new American Revue at the London Opera House has a good illustrated-paper kind of poster of a *Merveilleuse* lady, which

A Composition G. S. Lightfoot

Children Frances Jennings

The Palm Tree J. D. Innes

has only had an effect on me in one place. There is a certain wall in a main thoroughfare which proved too small for its length. The bill-sticker, concerned only to fulfil his functions, and caring nothing for anatomy, has folded up the bottom third of the picture, so that the lady's leg, attractively revealed by an aperture in her gown, grows out of her waist. This fascinated me, and when I saw the Revue I found that this poster gives a truer idea of the performance than its more fortunate duplicates do. At the London Opera House the ladies' legs do grow out of their waists, or, at least, such is my impression. They have a great many legs, but every attempt I made to count them was baffled, for they were for ever on the run, running out of nothing into nothing, aimlessly, without purpose, without humour, without zest. There was one period when I thought I should achieve my reckoning, but suddenly sixteen legs disappeared into a pool of water and I had to begin again, and before that I had been put out by the entertainment taking a sudden plunge into Max Reinhardt's Arabian Nights, so that I was forced into a curious contemplation of two pairs of male legs. Till then I had decided that the purpose of the entertainment was to display a large selection of female legs, but when I was presented with these four—two white and two stained brown—my ideas were upset and I was set wondering why four male legs should be enough for the female public of London while for the male public an unascertainable number should be necessary. This problem is still unsolved, though it remains interesting. There was no effective humour in the display, very little musical ability, no romance, no intelligence, hardly any of the qualities with which in musical comedy and English revues the appeal of legs is salted. Here, bluntly (and most expensively) was the stage used to satisfy that element in human nature upon which Mahommed founded a vision of Paradise. Less efficient than the One Prophet, the Americans responsible for this " colossal success " have bungled their use of their material and give the impression that female legs grow out of the female waist. Perhaps my friend the bill-sticker had seen the show and had been horrified into an access of honesty, for certainly his is the only poster that gives a correct idea of the new Revue, and it remains its aptest criticism.

A wicked spirit of irreverence almost drives me to wish that there were a few pairs of legs in *Strife*. Respect for the play and its author however win the day. The back-cloth of the speech scene in *Strife* is a picture of Welsh hills. These and the action that takes place among them call back to the mind that there are winds in the world, winds and foul weather and a hard living to be gained, harsh facts from which our townish huddling away leads us to take a dull delight in caps and bells and legs. To read the word *Strife* and the name John Galsworthy in the list of plays is to be braced to new hope. To attend the play is to have the comforting assurance that here at least is one man in the theatre who will not fawn upon his audience, or leer at it, or mewl at it, or strut before it, but one who to the best of his ability will in terms of the theatre set before his audience the facts that have stirred his emotion and by his art lead them into sharing his feeling, his desire, his warm perception of the forces that play about and through human action. He is an upright man that will not indulge in showman's tricks, nor mental tricks, nor make any appeal save through his art and the legitimate use of the machinery at his disposal. It is rather his sense of law and order than his sense of justice that will not let him allow his conflicting forces actually come to grips, and makes him state rather than reveal, deal with types rather than characters. That must be granted him. It is in his attitude, in his essence. What is so valuable is that within its scope his art is admirably disciplined, economical and effective. His is a stern wistfulness that is the most telling antidote to caps, bells and legs. These also are good things, admirable in their place, but, if they are not used in terms of the theatre they are as distasteful as any other raw material, as distasteful as Mr. Galsworthy's emotions would be, if he were ever slovenly enough to dump them down on the stage, without moulding them into form. Really the whole problem is resolved into a question of the right use and the wrong use of the theatre. Caps, bells and legs are every bit as good as wistful emotions if they are rightly used. The performance of *Strife* at the Comedy reveals an efficiency which is not to be found at any other theatre, except, perhaps, on a lower level, the Royalty. What a fortune that man will make who discovers the right use of legs in the theatre! Stravinsky and Fokin are very near it.

THEATRES IN THE AIR By JOHN DRINKWATER

MR. GORDON CRAIG ("Towards a New Theatre," Dent, 21*s*. net) has produced a beautiful book, and in that he justifies himself. If we complain that it fails in its primary intention we are ungracious, for the gift of a beautiful book can in no case be just cause for complaint, no matter how capricious its service may be. The imaginative reader of great dramatic literature is accustomed to create ideal performances in his mind, a visionary conduct of movement and conflict that is unimpeded by the thousand embarrassing circumstances of the theatre—mechanical difficulties and mishaps, the personality of the actor, the enormous problem of investing the complicated and delicate piece of machinery which is comprehensively called the stage with the freedom and elasticity of art. And he will, too, often set this ideal performance against an ideal background without consideration of time and space—of the theatre's walls. This background Mr. Craig does much to realise for us—on paper. These designs, with their admirable economy of detail and their stirring suggestion of height and distance cannot but leave our imagination the richer and more apt for the creation of those performances that outrun all the possibilities of theatrical device. Mr. Craig has dreamt well, and for this we are grateful. It may be said here that his new book is not greatly concerned with the opposition to words as the primary medium of drama that found an advocate in the author's "Art of the Theatre," and there is no present necessity to dispute Mr. Craig's denial of poetry on the stage. Many of these designs are made for accepted masterpieces of poetic drama, and whatever the designer's quarrel with the spoken word may be in general, it is not laboured here. Nor are we disposed to pay very much attention to the text of this present volume; Mr. Craig is not a good writer either in style or temperament. His prose is constantly apeing the ease of the conversational stylists, and always failing to catch their secret; it is rather like Mr. Newman or Mr. Montague on stilts, the fine lissomness of gait that is natural to them turning to awkward condescension, as who should walk a little way with Tom and Dick, poor fellows. There is, moreover, scarcely anything in these notes that was very much worth saying—rather an irritating wagging of the head with an "I could an if I would." So that dismissing the book as telling us but little of Mr. Craig's views of the whole art of the theatre and finding annoyance rather than pleasure in his writing, we are left with the bare designs themselves, which are indeed the sole—and ample—justification of the volume. We wish that they had been published in a folio without any trappings, but since their maker decided against this we are not disposed to quarrel unduly with what we take to be an indiscretion. These designs are full of imaginative beauty, and no one can look at them without realising that Mr. Craig is one of the most gifted men of his time. He has, as we have said, dreamt finely and cleanly; the imagination is never dissipated into mere fancy. But Mr. Craig calls his book "Towards a New Theatre," and it is at this point that the real trouble in his work begins.

A great play does not necessarily need the stage to prove its greatness, but it is certain that the dramatist can only achieve high mastery of construction by knowledge of, and in terms of, the theatre. It is questionable whether, apart from this gain, the artist can secure any profound and lasting pleasure from work in the theatre, but, however this may be, every artist who has any experience of such work knows that whatever the theatre may or may not be, it cannot possibly be a place of dreams. Life in a theatre is a life of continual conflict with immediate and practical difficulties on the stage, a daily compromise of ideals with necessity, of dreams with stubborn physical facts. The supreme virtue of the theatre is that it is the one instrument by which it is possible to make great art popular, and it is an understanding of this condition that is drawing so much of our best work to-day into its service. But the theatre is definitely a place in which to do and not to dream. Mr. Craig gives us a design for the last scene of the first act of *Hamlet.* It is extraordinarily impressive and really quickens our perception of the poet's mood. At the back of the stage is the figure of a man ; behind him rises a great square-cut block of building ; measuring this from our figure we find it to be sixty feet high, and the sky goes up above it. We do not see the full breadth of the scene, but measuring that part which is visible by the same standard we find it to be seventy-five feet—ninety feet if we allow a small margin on either side. It is, as we say, undeniably impressive, but will Mr. Craig put it on a stage for us ? We have another design : a dark flight of steps—thirty-five steps as nearly as we can count them ; a foreground of perhaps ten feet. On the steps is the figure of a woman, an isolated point of light in the surrounding darkness. Mr. Craig sees much emotional value in the design, and so do we ; will he put it on a stage for us ? It does not help us to tell us that he is working towards *a* new theatre and not *the* new theatre. The fact is that there is not the remotest possibility of a theatre in which these designs could be translated into terms of the actual stage. You cannot have sixty-feet high buildings with the sky over them on the stage, and if you could you would have a stage that would be useless for everything but pantomime. And you cannot light a single figure without lighting a surrounding space. At least, you cannot do these things in the theatre that is already beginning to announce again that it will have its own passionate and vigorous life, whatever might be done in the theatre towards which Mr. Craig tells us he is pointing, saying gaily that it is also a mountain. Of course many things might be done in or on a mountain, but that is another matter. The young theatre to-day is in fierce opposition to a misconceived and wholly unpoetic principle of stage decoration. Mr. Craig, more perhaps than any man living, might lead and inspirit it in a struggle that means a good many bruises ; or he may quite justly absent himself from the theatre altogether and continue to achieve admirable designs which will feed the imagination but not the stage. If he is to do us the former service he must show us how to work in cloth and wood and limes and electric bulbs, remembering that the people who are willing to have their imaginations stirred and to pay for the adventure will not fill a mountain ; that the theatre, in other words, insists before everything else that the artist shall oppose himself to practical difficulties at every turn and that he prove every dream upon the stage as he goes along. It is not surprising that many artists, realising these severities of the theatre, refuse to bow to a discipline so stern. If Mr. Craig confessed himself to be of these, nobody could blame him, and his art would lose nothing. But it is useless to tell us that he is pointing the way to achievements in the theatre which even he himself, by his own witness, can yet do little more than see dimly in rapt ecstasy, and at the same time ignore the perplexing but inflexible conditions that the theatre imposes on its servants.

POETRY

By LASCELLES ABERCROMBIE

"Thou hast made me endless, such is thy pleasure."

IT is hard to keep clear of the critical King Cambyses' vein when one has to write about Rabindra Nath Tagore's "Gitanjali" (Macmillan 4s. 6d. net.). "Thou hast made me endless . . ." Yes, that is the danger. It is, I suppose, one of the paradoxes of æsthetics, that poetry, when it achieves a perfect formality—when form and impulse are inevitably related—has the power of causing a notable sense of complete liberation from all the formality of consciousness: "Thou hast made me endless." Life can get nothing better than these moments; they belong to Dionysus. But they are "unexpressive." The making of great poetry is a transformation of Dionysus into Apollo; but the reading of great poetry is a transformation of Apollo back into Dionysus. And Dionysus untransformed is still less the god of criticism than he is of poetry. He is, however, the god of King Cambyses' vein, which, as a good European, I am bound to detest above everything. As a precaution against him—to give him time for settling down into the everyday formality of thought—I shall speculate a little about the significance of "Gitanjali" outside of art. For Tagore's work belongs to world-politics as well as to poetry. As I read his own exquisite prose translation of his songs, I seem to have jumped right over that formidable clash which is, or ought to be, at the back of everybody's mind—the coming clash of East and West; I seem to have landed magically in its serene and triumphant conclusion. All the great original civilisations of the world (including the one on whose bequests we are still living) have resulted from the East fusing somehow with the West. And always it has been the East that supplied impulse—Dionysus, the West that supplied form—Apollo; for the resulting triumph of vitality, each was as necessary as the other. Now this seems to me exactly what has happened afresh in "Gitanjali." The book is not only noble poetry; it is a new civilisation. This is why it is so incomprehensibly surprising. When one is talking of poetry, Dionysus and Apollo will always come in very conveniently as figures of speech ; that is how I was using them just now. But in " Gitanjali " they have become gods once more. A profound impulse from the East and a masterful formality from the West have joined together to create a new perfection of conscious life.

This, at any rate, is how I read the book. And there seems no doubt that it actually is a joint product of East and West. Rabindra Nath Tagore's family has long been conspicuous for its efforts to Europeanise India, or Indianise Europe, whichever you prefer. His father took a great part in establishing the Brahma Samaj, an eclectic theistic religion which appears to have deliberately attempted to compound the formal thought of the West with Indian spiritual intuition. I believe it has had an immense influence. But the real result of the Brahma Samaj is in the songs of Rabindra Nath Tagore, which have penetrated the whole of Indian life. I may be hunting a chimæra ; but really this seems to me extraordinarily significant. Compare these songs with almost any other Eastern poetry, and you will see what I mean. Eastern poetry, however, means for most of us, I suppose, Fitzgerald's Omar ; and the comparison here will not be so striking. For Fitzgerald " tampered," as they say, with his original : in fact, he turned it into a European poem. Read a literal translation of Omar, and you will see that Fitzgerald gave to his original just that which is so noticeably supreme in " Gitanjali " : he gave it form. But Hafiz will show how Tagore differs from typical Oriental lyrics. No one can miss the puissance of impulse in Hafiz ; but I imagine that most Europeans would agree that it is impossible to read Hafiz with any comfort, not even in a reading that so admirably suggests the external form as Walter Leaf's translation. What disturbs us is the complete lack of internal form agreeing with the external. Orientalists, of course, admit this ; they say Persian poetry (and it is evidently true of Eastern poetry in general) gets its unity and only professes to get it, from an extraordinarily strict externality of form : the spirit within the poetry is " free." That is merely to say, the spirit is shapeless ; and as long as Greece lives in Europe, we are not likely to be satisfied with shapeless spirit, however shapely the substance may be. A more familiar instance, doubtless, would be the Canticles; and their purport is very close to that of " Gitanjali." The inspiration of the Canticles is as sublime as anything in poetry; but it is utterly shapeless. It is ungoverned; Dionysus has not contrived to turn into Apollo.

And that is just what he has contrived to do in " Gitanjali." I certainly should not compare the inspiration of this book with the depth and splendour of the inspiration of Hafiz or the Canticles. It does not seem, like theirs, a rage from the very heart of life. It is finer, more delicate, more wistful, decidedly less profound. But all the same, compared with modern European poetry, it amazingly seems to have behind it the pressure of vast reservoirs of vitality. No doubt this comes from the immense force of Indian religion. The thing is, however, that this elemental kind of inspiration has been mastered into complete formality as shapely and exquisite as anything in the whole range of European lyric; and, I think, considering the facts of the milieu in which " Gitanjali " originated, we may truly call this formality Western. But whether this be so or not, it makes Tagore's poetry of the same nature as the poetry of Sappho or Simonides, Wordsworth or Heine; and —here is the amazing thing—this without ceasing to be altogether Oriental and Indian. The translation of " Gitanjali " gives us, of course, no notion of the external form of these songs; but it must certainly be something beautiful. Beauty of external form by no means compels the spirit within to be shapely: it may easily be " free," or shapeless. But " soul is form and doth the body make ": when the soul *is* form—when thought and mood have such superb shapeliness as they have in " Gitanjali "—the body cannot refuse obedience to it.

It is possible that the Brahma Samaj—and by that I mean the " contamination " of East and West—may be responsible for Tagore's noble mingling of mystical aspiration with a profound and delighted acceptance of life. But probably this is simply the result of Tagore's genius; for mysticism in Europe has always been just as inclined to deny life as mysticism in the East. In any case, the quality is one of the chief things in what Mr. Ransome would call the " kinetic " of the book—in what it sets out to say. But I shall not attempt the futility of describing what " Gitanjali " is like. In the bounty and glow and simplicity of its imagery, it is as if it discovers vitality itself. But it is more than a deep flux of vitality; it is vitality daring to hold itself in a supreme consciousness. The forces of its inspiration have made themselves into lucid formality, like the forces that build crystals; and therefore it is poetry that can as easily and as equally speak of strange and remote experiences of the spirit as of the divine lusts of the senses. Just because, I believe, it promises a new civilisation, but promises it in the old way, in another fusion of the spiritual energy of the East with the mental formality of the West—just because of this, it is poetry which once more achieves the condition towards which all poetry is for ever straining: it is a perfection of conscious life.

Well, I hope I have avoided King Cambyses' vein; I am not quite sure. But I shall have no difficulty in keeping clear of it for the rest of this article. Not that " Gitanjali," as an earnest of future wonders, need make us desperate about the present. We are not doing so badly ourselves; after Tagore's Indian dream, we need not cry to dream again. Indeed, if we had several books like Mr. D. H. Lawrence's " Love-Poems " (Duckworth 4s. 6d. net), I should certainly have to say that we are doing astonishingly well. But, though Mr. Masefield's " Dauber " (Heinemann 3s. 6d. net) has appeared in book form, Mr. Lawrence's poems stand by themselves, among recent books, for justifiable daring. " Dauber " seems to me the least successful of Mr. Masefield's narratives; chiefly because only a rattling good story could justify a poem of such length, and the story is a very poor affair; it is false in psychology and false in sentiment. The hero's death ought to have been significant; but I cannot help suspecting that Mr.

Masefield, having turned his hero at last into a decent sort of chap, killed him because he did not know what to do with him. Even so, however, there are several pages of incomparable description, and continual lightning flashes of splendid phrasing. But I do not like having to praise Mr. Masefield only for the ornament of his poetry. I cannot find much to say either about Mr. Hewlett's " Helen Redeemed " (Macmillan 4s. 6d. net) or Mr. William Watson's " The Muse in Exile." Since Mr. Hewlett published " Artemision," his verse seems to have been trying hard to recapture the qualities which enabled that delightful book to do something considerable towards the poetic re-creation of Greek legend. One cannot but admire the determined Hellenism of this confirmed romantic. Only in one poem in this latest book of his—in " Gnatho "—can I find anything comparable with the keen phrasing and vivid conception of " Artemision." The rest is what you might expect from the industry of a romantic trying to be a Hellenist. Of Mr. Watson's " The Muse in Exile " (Jenkins 3s. 6d. net) I will not say anything at all ; I have too much respect for Mr. Watson's past. Miss Emilia Stuart Lorimer's " Songs of Alban " (Constable 3s. 6d. net) is another book I must pass by. Her writing is evidently quite alive ; but I find it difficult to enjoy poetry which I cannot understand ; and there is very little of Miss Lorimer's which I can understand.

So I am left with Mr. Lawrence's " Love Poems." There is novelty here ; but the right sort of novelty. It is poetry realising things afresh. If " realist " were not a word abominably misused, it would be the word for Mr. Lawrence's poems. I do not care very much for his rhythms ; their daring seems to be really a fear of being conventional, though sometimes, as when he uses monosyllabic feet, they are obviously effective :

> " To ha'e gone an' given his white young flesh
> To a woman that coarse."

And the love in his " Love Poems " is rather too monotonously the " bitter-sweet impracticable adder." But Mr. Lawrence has an admirable power of liberating the concealed meaning of words, and an equally admirable power of unexpected but truthful association. These lines give an instance of both these qualities :

" a grey pale light like must
That settled upon my face and hands till it seemed
To flourish there, as pale mould blooms on a crust."

The choice of the word " flourish " marks Mr. Lawrence as a poet ; and a sinister dawn is captured with curious assurance by the suggestion, physical as well as emotional, of mould. Such detail as this Mr. Lawrence uses for the patient, elaborate and extraordinarily economical fixation of a sequence of moods which, for all that they are somewhat monotonous, are so concentrated into poetry that they are quite irresistible. But, remarkable as these " love poems " are, Mr. Lawrence works with less effort, and to clearer result, in the sharp psychology and vigorously restrained word-play of the dialect poems at the end of his book.

THE NOVELS By HUGH WALPOLE

Imagination

THE use of the imagination has been complicated for the modern novelist by the emphasis laid by the modern critic upon the importance of recorded observation. It was at one time demanded that Mr. Micawber and Becky Sharp should not only have sharply defined dwellings and properties of a very recognisable kind, but that they should also, of themselves, be individual and memorable characters. Now that background is of itself almost sufficient to claim approving attention, and the fact that one can remember the angles of the playground at one's board-school and the exact appearance of the counter at the shop where one was once an eager assistant is enough to catch the critics and readers by the throat.

Mr. Wells and Mr. Arnold Bennett, who have, in their sharp retention of experience, enough material to last them until the end of their days, have nevertheless produced some of their most remarkable work by the fine energy of their imagination; the deserted London in "The War of the Worlds" and the execution in "The Old Wives' Tale" are as powerful and as true as the experiences of Kipps or the aspirations of young Clayhanger.

The lesser novelist of to-day, however, betrays at every step that his imagination is consciously fettered by the close proximity of his public. Unless he is of the first rank, and artist enough to give this same imagination precedence to this cherished public, one success will kill his spontaneity, strangle his honesty, weaken his individuality; here in Mr. W. J. Locke's "Stella Maris" (John Lane, 6s.) is pertinent and distressing evidence of this. There are many who admired the books that Mr. Locke gave to the world before "Marcus Ordeyne" as work of the very finest promise and of considerable performance. "The Usurper," "Where Love Is," "The White Dove," these were individual, honest, admirable studies in character. Yvonne in "Derelicts" and the Lanyons in "The White Dove" are etchings of the most brilliant order. With "Marcus Ordeyne" came popular success and, since then, so anxious has been Mr. Locke to give his public what they wish him to give them, that spontaneity of imagination has been utterly and recklessly abandoned. In " Stella Maris," the latest and surely the worst of his novels, we can behold this shackled imagination struggling at first, ultimately defeated, imprisoned, abandoned.

The idea of someone, living away from the world, innocent, happy, ignorant, plunged then, suddenly, into experience and beaten to the ground with the shock of it, is, if not absolutely new, packed with possibilities. I believe that, at the beginning, Mr. Locke saw these possibilities, but saw also that an honest development of them would have forbidden both that sentimentality and that crudity that his public now expect from him. His imagination protests. " Come," says Mr. Locke, " you've got to do what I tell you—no more nonsense." We have then a beautiful girl with " a pair of frail arms, a daintily curved neck, a haunting face, and a mass of dark hair encircling it on the pillow like a nimbus." We have a strong rugged hero, a wonderful villainess, thin-lipped and always dressed in black, a charity child, surely related to Little Nell and Little Paul. The psychological interest of the effect upon Stella of the revelation of a wicked (here a purple) world is sunk beneath such sentences as " The cruel, vulgar and hideous things of life were not the appanages of a class apart. They entered into her own narrowed world. Her beautiful world! Her hateful, horrible terror of a world!" or " Stella rose, and clasping hands to her bosom, went to him—

" ' Belovedest, for Christ's sake, what is the end of all this?' "

The end of it all is, of course:

" He put his arm around her, and all his love spoke. ' You. The living mystery of beauty that is you.' He whispered into her lips. ' You—Stella Maris—Star of the Sea!' "

There is no humour in this book.

If Mr. Locke has chained his Imagination for fear of the things that it might do, Miss Mayer in " The Third Miss Symons "

(Sidgwick, 3s. 6d. net) has discarded it altogether. Here I must frankly admit that Mr. Masefield's eulogistic preface aroused too eager an excitement. In this preface he says : " The world is, of course, the comparatively passive feminine world, but few modern books (if any) have treated of that world so happily, with such complete acceptance, unbiassed and unprejudiced, yet with such selective tact and variety of gaiety." Remembering the work of Mrs. Wharton, Anne Douglas Sedgwick, Miss Sinclair, Miss Cholmondeley, Miss Ethel Sidgwick and others, all of whom have had for their stage this " comparatively passive feminine world," I was naturally determined to judge " The Third Miss Symons " by high standards. To these standards Miss Mayer's little book does not begin to attain. Here is an accurate, well-written, grey, narration of a melancholy spinster's passage through the world. The observation is accurate, the atmosphere of heavy chandeliers, mid-day Sunday beef, and grey gloves worn at the finger-tips, most carefully maintained. Here is this material waiting for Imagination to come and start it into flame. Imagination never comes. The facts are there, the observation is accurate, and from it all nothing is to be gathered, nothing carries, in its spontaneous vitality, any relation to the other victories, the other tragedies that life can show. No, observation is not enough.

Here, indeed, in another first novel, published in the same month, is Mr. Masefield's too eager statement immediately contradicted. Miss Ivy Low in " Growing Pains " (Heinemann, 6s.) has, for her study, this same " passive feminine world " and in it she does not entirely disregard the claims of Imagination, does produce something that has life and colour somewhere at its heart. It is in the earlier portion of her book that Miss Low is most successful. Her nervous, self-centred morbid little girl, flying from temper to affection, from bulls'-eyes (stolen out of a shop) to religion, is most admirably described, and Miss Low does use her imagination sufficiently to place this little girl in relation with all the other things in a restless and agitated world. In the book there is poetry, too, and a very admirable humour. Miss Low has not, as yet, learnt the lessons of construction and development, but hers is the best first novel that the present year has yet produced.

Imagination, if it has not accompanied Miss Low quite far enough, has yielded to Miss Ethel Sidgwick almost too bountifully. In " Succession " (Sidgwick and Jackson, 6s.), we are given the long-expected sequel to " Promise " and are faced at the book's close by the question as to why this world that Miss Sidgwick has herself seen so vividly and given to us so bountifully, a world full of pathos, humour, and excitement, is ultimately for us so difficult of comprehension.

There is no doubt here of the fulness and vigour of Miss Sidgwick's imagination nor of the freedom and authority that she has given to it, so that she has simply followed and written as it has commanded her. But Miss Sidgwick's book is difficult to read because the author, in the desire to give her imagination its finest freedom, has refused, when the career is run and the adventure is concluded, any final and eliminating revision. There the plunder that her excursion has provided for her is lying ; from this plunder there should be selection, discipline, order. The story of the struggle of the soul of a genius against physical weakness is fine, the crowd of persons protecting, assaulting this genius, is admirably described and illuminated. Only from the great mass of dialogue, from the piling of minutiæ upon minutiæ, from the constant iteration of the Parisian and Munich background, enough does not finally reward the reader. The boy, his grandfather, his uncle, the composers, the other musicians, his philistine father, are there and are truthfully there, but their capture has been difficult and even when the tale is ended, the mists are still about them.

Mr. Beresford's " Goslings " (Heinemann, 6s.) on the other hand, is almost too rigorously pruned, and this only because the invention is so lively, the characters so admirably vital that every reader will wish that the book had been twice as long. Here, truly, is imagination rightly disciplined.

Mr. Beresford, in his story of a plague that swept over Europe and left, for the most part, only women behind it, betrays all the philosophical acuteness and original invention that we should expect from the author of " The Hampdenshire Wonder " and also a colour and poetry that have been lacking in his earlier books.

His picture of a deserted London will call to mind Mr. Wells' " War of the Worlds," but even here Mr. Beresford has much that is his own. That vast empty street with the mad " Queen of the Earth " shining with stolen jewels, shouting as she goes, for its only inhabitant, will not be easily forgotten by Mr. Beresford's readers. But it is in his second part that his imagination is most surely and emphatically original. His women—old Mrs. Gosling, the two girls, Eileen, Elsie Durham and the rest—are so sharply defined, and open up, in their relations to one another, so many novel and thrilling developments, that the history of their adventures is all too short.

Poor Mrs. Gosling is most triumphantly distinguished against the bizarrerie and fantastic colour of the background. " No doubt our 'Eavenly Father will make excuses " is her wavering resort to some half-remembered security and, against the garlanded debauchery of the Butcher of High Wycombe and the invasions of Pan into a new relaxing civilisation, such security was badly needed.

" Goslings " is the most vital book that Mr. Beresford has given us; here then is Imagination, not, as with Mr. Locke, discarded, nor, as with Miss Sidgwick, undisciplined, but honestly developed and bravely restrained.

GENERAL LITERATURE By FRANK SWINNERTON

Gretton's Modern History, A Small Boy, Steps to Parnassus, Lore of Proserpine, Dreams.

NO particular descriptive term has in general been for years so commonly misunderstood as the word "detachment." Writers dealing with the kind of fictional art condemned as "realism" have always supposed that "realism" meant something laboriously objective, whereas "realism" (for which I am told writers to the *Westminster Gazette* have been trying to find a more apologetic name) is not necessarily either laborious or objective, once it is properly mastered by the realist and his critics. English realism does not set up a convention of not knowing anything about subjective states: it is, on the contrary, primarily concerned with a revolt against material things, by the extraordinarily simple means of showing how they very evilly dominate the lives of the majority of men. And it is ironic, and genuinely detached. Now the reason it so clearly indicates its true succession to the older school of English writers is that the detachment of English realism is—not objectivity, but a very quiet, typically English, humorous judgment. English realism, then, is intellectual to the extent that it is based upon lucid judgment; but its detachment is nothing more nor less than the peculiar focussing power of this critical humour, which makes it unheroical and, I hope, unsentimental, but never insensitive. And it is not restricted to fiction, because realism is an attitude of mind, and not simply a technical method.

Mr. Gretton, in his "Modern History of the English People, 1880–1910" (Grant Richards, 2 vols., 7*s*. 6*d*. net each), of which the second volume is now published, is witty rather than ironic, because he is a serious and responsible annalist; but his detachment is entirely admirable. His book is not so much a history as a gloss upon events, and it is sometimes a little difficult in the absence of consecutive narrative to emulate Mr. Gretton's alertness in springing from subject to subject. But, apart from that fact, and the further fact that the extreme conciseness of the book demands the assumption by Mr. Gretton of the reader's familiarity with such things as the financial world and its vocabulary, the " follow-on " rule, and the qualities of Harris tweed, the two volumes have a clearness as well as a critical value and a humour of the highest significance. The writing is wonderfully brief and efficient, avoiding both baldness and overloading : the difficulty of compression and selection has been overcome with immense gusto. The omission of references to the Kinema has been noted elsewhere : I may perhaps mention two other very slight points. " De Rougemont," I believe, was not a real name ; and the *Daily Mirror* was not really started as a halfpenny photographic daily. It was intended as a penny newspaper for " ladies," and adopted its present form after a short run on its first lines.

Very different from Mr. Gretton's work, and from each other, are the two books recently promulgated by distinguished novelists, though both deal autobiographically with the early years of life. Mr. Henry James, beginning with the idea that the public would like to have early recollections of his brother, William James, has been able to re-create with characteristic detachment the world in which they both moved as boys. Not many of these pages deal actually with W. J., but they are nevertheless a perfect delight, as wonderful as pages from Mr. James's most wonderful novels, and throwing off the same fascinating air of the understanding of a unique order of life. It is a delight, especially, to catch in delicious long miraculously-sustained and completed sentences, the very real history of Mr. James's progress to comprehension of his own " subtle " perception of things, which he styles a virtue and then, against himself, admits a vice. How, from the time when an aunt forbade her little girl to " make a scene," his mind began to see everything in scenes and situations, to the time when he realised that " everything should represent something more than what immediately and all too blankly met the eye," his progress to the possession of the true power of observation and retention is here disclosed. As the picture of a novelist in his earliest stages, " A

Small Boy, and Others " (Macmillan, 12s. net) is fascinating to the lover of that novelist. As a beautiful picture in its own right, which " glimmers at me as out of a thin golden haze, with all the charm, for imagination and memory, of pressing pursuit rewarded, of distinctness in the dimness, of the flush of life in the grey, of the wonder of consciousness in everything "—so impossible it is better to express the impression of the book than in Mr. James's own words—it is a supreme and delightful work of art, based upon truth humorously observed, in the best English tradition. Mr. James's detachment is nowhere illustrated more surely; the inexpressible candour of his primary perceptions, made difficult for us only by the consummate analysis of their interplay, is here once again revealed. Making observation the corner-stone of his art, " pedestrian gaping having been in childhood," Mr. James says, " prevailingly my line," embalmed, as it were, " in a sort of fatalism of patience," he presently seems to define art as " dignity and memory and measure," " conscience and proportion and taste, not to mention strong sense too." And if that is the definition of art, then surely Mr. James establishes his right for ever to be regarded as one of the most " artistic " artists who have ever lived. Whatever may be his ultimate position among novelists, his influence upon novelists of the present day is probably greater than that of any other writer of any time. It is impossible, that is to say, not to learn from Mr. James—sometimes the peculiarity of his later style, but inevitably something of the vital sense of truth that pervades his books, however his later conventions may have strayed from the clarity of " Roderick Hudson " and the exquisite " Portrait of a Lady." Mr. James, like all other realists, has never shrunk from the full exercise of his most fastidious perceptions. For that virtue alone he deserves canonisation: he has never preached; but has always found the complexities and simplicities of life his absorbing study. And if we would judge the almost ingenuous manner of his sensitive approach to impressions, we are bound to read " A Small Boy " with gratitude and affectionate delight.

Mr. J. C. Squire (" Steps to Parnassus," Latimer, 3*s*. 6*d*. net) does not shrink from his perceptions ; but a parodist such as Mr. Squire deserves something to parody. To ridicule the mediocre is one of the most useless occupations in life ; and it is almost intolerable to see a man of Mr. Squire's quite especial talent doing wilfully what his victims fumblingly do in all good faith. So these " Steps to Parnassus " are more by way of being cruelly humorous imitations than parodies : in the case of Mr. Masefield, apart from the sublime lapse into poetry, after Mr. Masefield's own manner, the fun is too boisterous and unlike to be amusing. Elsewhere it is not really very edifying to have one's contempt for the jejune roused by Mr. Squire's malicious pleasure in emulation.

Different indeed from any of the other books notable this month is " Lore of Proserpine " (Macmillan, 5*s*. net), for it is by no means humorous, or even very entertaining. " You will gather," says Mr. Maurice Hewlett, " that I was a reader." Either that, or the cult of fairies is but a sad one, for this jaded, unhappy, sterile book is otherwise inexplicable. No grace is here, no tender delicate participation in what we might assume to be the exquisiteness of the fairy realm. Instead, we find fairies very prosaic little persons, clad invariably in a single respectable garment (which, however, seems not quite to suffice in cold weather to keep the owner warm); and Mr. Hewlett is not at all moved to any lightness of touch. After twice conducting us through the books which he (in common with nearly every other boy) read in early years, he tells us about the solemn little fairies he has seen, and repeats two long stories —one of a fairy visitant and babe-stealer, the other of a fairy wife— in which his own experience is not concerned. But in all these stories, even in that of the Oreads in Wiltshire, there is a commonplaceness of imagining, no less than a hardness of relation, which is really astonishing. It is as though Mr. Hewlett had determined to put aside all his various mantles—such as those which yielded the beautiful " Earthwork out of Tuscany," the incomparably rich " Forest Lovers," the harsher novels of actual history, and the more recent experiments in modern romance—and show to our unwilling gaze the secret reason why these splendidly costumed works, each swaggering in a richly embroidered cloak of brilliant phrases, never seemed, in all their dazzling wonder, to have truly operative hearts. He has essayed realism, the writing of things strongly seen and felt in a style of convincing simplicity ; and the effect is one of a book which is neither lively (as we might surely expect it to be) nor scientific. Mr. Hewlett would not have it scientific : nor would we. But if he is to adopt recognised poetic names, such as Queen Mab, and Oberon, and, presumably, the fairy " common herd " (as he seems to do), he should also, I should have supposed, make his accounts less laborious and more spirited, in the manner of the poets from whom he borrows his nomenclature. As it is, the fairies in " Lore of Proserpine " are simply unpleasing and substantial creatures such as we may see at any time in daylight without excitement, and if they are as dull as this, there seems no actual virtue in acquaintance with them. Moreover, the book has a horrible number of banalities, such as " Every one of us lives in a guarded house ; door shut, windows curtained " ; " We are bound—all of us—by our natures, bound by them and bounded " ; and, worst of all, " *The Forsaken Merman* is a beautiful poem, but not a safe guide to those who would relate the ways of the spirits of the sea." Surely the book is a subject for Mr. Squire !

Mr. Reginald Hine (" Dreams and the Way of Dreams," Dent, 5*s*. net) has produced a very agreeable miscellany of dreams, and quotations from all sorts of authors, ancient and modern, and exceedingly apt and humorous remarks of his own. The dreams given are in some cases serious, and in others the strange chaotic medleys that cause so much laughter at the breakfast table ; but all are good. Mr. Hine writes from his own experience, and is so far scientific ; and he has a tremendous familiarity with what has been written upon the subject. He is a genuine believer in the value and the truth of dreams and dreaming ; but he is no bigot. That is to say, he is a humourist, and is therefore able to see himself and his enthusiasm with detachment, even while, none the less, believing firmly in what he has to say. Accordingly his book is one to be enjoyed on quite other grounds than the mere discussion of the author's case, which perhaps is less important than his very nice dreams. But Mr. Hine is a good writer as well as a good dreamer, and he has a mighty commonplace-book from which he culls pleasant quotations.

Looking back over this chronicle, I hope I have not laboured the word " detachment " too hard. I have found the quality in all the books save one, and in that one I judge it to be absent because humour is absent from the author's essential make-up. Mr. Hewlett's modern comedies are quite obviously based upon an artificial convention rather than a truly ironic conception of life. They make, indeed, hardly any pretence of representing life, and must be judged by their own convention. But when Mr. Hewlett brings his hobby into the open, and rides it with a prim solemnity, it is surely permissible to call his book a dull book ? And it is dull because he is too seriously intent upon it : he has the feeling of being a seer. " I take leave to flatter myself," he says, " that my own will be indispensable Prolegomena to any such work [a study of the Præternatural], or to any research tending to its compilation." That sentence offends me precisely because it reveals absorption untempered by either poetic enthusiasm or true detachment. One can't even be sure that it is true.

FRENCH BOOKS By JOHN MIDDLETON MURRY

A Classical Revival

THERE are perhaps two reasons why the younger generation of French writers is given to collective introspection and absorbed in speculation upon tendencies. The first is the economic fact that one of the easiest and least costly methods of procuring copy for a *revue jeune* is to conduct an *enquête;* the second is that for better or worse the French logical mind is prone to develop a mania for literary classification and a disregard for the essential characteristics of the subject matter of the classification—literature. Consequently, it is very difficult to derive any real information from so extensive an inquiry as that of MM. Picard and Muller (" Les Tendances Présentes de la Litterature Française." Basset. 3 fr. 50). Even if the classification into grandiose schools, *Unanimistes*, *Paroxystes* and the like, is admitted by the writers themselves, the labels tell us nothing, for they are concerned with the accidents rather than the essentials of literature ; much as though we decided to base our own literary criticism upon a division of modern Poets into those who eat bacon and eggs for breakfast and those who do not. Chaotic classification is a delusion and a snare. More satisfactory, because more restricted and definite, is the inquiry conducted by M. Emile Henriot in *Le Temps* (" A Quoi rêvent les Jeunes Gens ? " Champion. 2 fr.) ; yet even here, if we consider the replies as a whole, the result is negative. The young French writers of to-day have completely broken with Symbolism ; and if the contributors to M. Henriot's symposium are unanimous in affirming that there is no " new school," they are unanimous no less in denying the gods of the nineties.

The desire for novelty at all costs is no longer characteristic of young French literature ; and the generation which expressed this desire in *vers libre* and sought its models in America, in Germany, in Flanders, in any country save France itself, is past. It is true that any evolution from the artistic position taken up by Mallarmé was of itself doomed to sterility ; but other causes than a mere æsthetic impossibility have been at work. It would be difficult to overestimate the literary importance of the foundation of the political organisation, *L'Action Française*, with its royalist and Catholic programme and its watchword " France for the French." The immediate cause of the *Action Française* was the Dreyfus trial, and though English opinion was practically unanimous in supporting Dreyfus and condemning anti-Semitism, there can be little doubt that on purely nationalist grounds the French agitation against Dreyfus was justified. A French nationalist policy, such as that adopted by the *Action Française* demands that France should remain a Catholic country and that its government should not rest in the hands of naturalised Jews or other aliens. Although it may seem that the growing popularity of such a party has no immediate connection with the literary tendencies of modern France, the connecting link is supplied by two individuals, Maurice Barrès and Charles Maurras. Catholic in their sympathies, nationalist in their politics, classical in their literary descent, Maurice Barrès as the creative artist, Charles Maurras as the critic, enjoy an influence which becomes every day more widespread. From Charles Maurras descends the most powerful of the younger critical groups to-day, that of the *Revue Critique*. The political programme of the *Action Française* is translated into literary terms. Alien influence must be excluded from French literature ; a return to the truest French tradition, to Racine, Pascal, Lafontaine, Stendhal, to Villon and to the Pléiade, must be exacted by the new criticism. We have only to compare Charles Maurras' latest book, " La Politique Religieuse " (Nouvelle Libraire Nationale, 3 fr. 50), in which the Catholic anti-alien policy is argued with the author's accustomed purity of style and language, with " Les Disciplines," by M. Henri Clonard (Rivière, 3 fr. 50), the chief critic of the *Revue Critique*, to see how close is the connection between the classical renaissance in politics and in literature. The authority of M. Maurras is quoted again and again in M. Clouard's book ; the very sub-title, " La Necessité littéraire et sociale d'une renaissance classique " reads like a phrase of the master's. The burden of the argument is pure Maurras. Romanticism must be forgotten, and the German prophets who preached it rejected for the true French tradition. " An imagination," says M. Clouard, " can very well be happy and brilliant, a point of view picturesque, a sentiment beautiful. But if you substitute them for analysis and experience where there are no other possible intermediaries between man and reality, you are mistaken and deceived on every hand." Analysis and experience—they are the old characteristics of French classicism and the ideals of the renaissance in France to-day.

It is symptomatic that a recent number of the *Revue Critique* was entirely devoted to Stendhal, in whom the analytic genius of French literature reached perhaps its highest development; while soon after *Les Marches de Provence* devoted a whole number to the consideration of *fantaisie et fantaisistes*. The *Fantaisistes* form a new school of French poets, with this striking difference from the generality of schools, that they have no programme or propaganda, no pseudo-philosophical theory of life on which to wreck their poetry. " Fantasy " in the sense in which the *Fantaisistes* use it for their watchword is a quality of temperament and not an æsthetic dogma ; it is the faculty of analysing experience with an irony that verges on cynicism and an introspection that verges on egotism. In short, " fantasy " has always been an eminently French quality, in spite of the fact that its literary expression has been borne down for centuries by foreign influences, Spanish in the seventeenth century, English in the eighteenth, and German in the nineteenth. The terrible irony of Villon, the titanic imagination of Rabelais—these are the purely French products of fantasy. Jules Laforgue was a genius of the same mould. To this essentially French tradition many of the most significant of the younger generation attach themselves, P. J. Toulet, Tristan Derème, Francis Carco, Jean-Marc Bernard, Jean Pellerin, to name the most significant ; and to this tradition belong three slender books of poetry, " Le Poème de la Pipe et de l'Escargot," by Tristan Derème, " Chansons Aigres-Douces," by Francis Carco (Collection des Cinq), " Sub Tegmine Fagi," by Jean-Marc Bernard (Editions du Temps Présent, 3 fr. 50). The title of M. Carco's book applies to all three ; they are all bitter-sweet. There is a delicate irony and a wonderful perfection of form in all, and underneath there seems to lurk a profound malaise. I am not here concerned to detach the individuality of these three poets ; but rather to emphasise their common quality. Here is poetry that is sure at least of its own ground, and sure of its essentially French spirit. It is poetry that does not thrust a theory of the universe into a lyric, nor disdain a perfection of form which is the birth-right of French poetry. Though as yet the *Fantaisistes* have no great body of work to their credit, they have at least this recommendation to our serious consideration, that they do not thunder before they have learned to speak, while they have jettisoned the preposterous cargo of " -ismes " under which young French poetry has laboured for twenty years. M. Derème has the secret of a real Poetry when he writes :

Ma vie en silence s'écoule
C'est pour peu d'hommes que j'écris
Car si je chantais pour la foule
Je pousserais bien d'autres cris.

Des deux poings défiant les astres
Je clamerais a grand fracas
Et ferais crouler les pilastres
Et les balustres sur mes pas

. . . . .

Et peut-être dans mon vieil âge
Pourrais-je voir sur mon perron
Un laurier bercer son feuillage
Mais à quoi bon ? mais à quoi bon ?

There has lately been too much conscious " shaking fists at the stars " in French poetry, and the time has come for a classical revival after the anarchy and cosmopolitanism of recent years. A classical revival does not involve denying the last century and a half. Romanticism is in the French blood now as it is in ours. A classical revival means putting things in their place. In the pregnant phrase of M. J.-M. Bernard, Romanticism is but an element of literature ; classicism is a principle.

RECENT FRENCH NOVELS By X. MARCEL BOULESTIN

IF it is true that the French Drama is at present in a state of decadence or, at least, of stagnation, it is none the less true that many French novels are now written that show not only remarkable cleverness and wonderful display of technique, but also a broader view of Life and a passionate interest in things of vital importance.

During the last decade most French writers wrote books dealing only with love and *adultère* (or even *adultère* without love) and their consequences, pleasant or unpleasant; but it seems now as if a reaction had really begun. And it is a sign of the times that the present year has seen the birth of such books as *L'Ordination*, *Cauët*, *Vieille Histoire* and *La Colline inspirée*. Moreover these are not exceptional instances, for three of the works with which I am now concerned present the same characteristics : human interest, observation of real life and emotional appeal outside the relation of the sexes.

Mme. Colette Willy's new book, *L'Envers du Music-Hall* (Flammarion, 3 fr. 50), for instance, shows us the *monde* of the lower French music-halls, from the hard-working, honest acrobat to the chorus-girl of the up-to-date Revue, *monde* of which we had already a glimpse in *La Vagabonde*. Only this time no psychological plot and delicate *sentimentalités* are there to distract our attention from the sometimes depressing realities of that special kind of stage life. Colette Willy can see and she can describe, and through the medium of her talent, we can see them too, those artists of the music-halls, " off " without their make-up, their graceful gestures and their fine clothes—as they really are. These sketches are sometimes very amusing, often very pathetic, and always admirably done. For Colette Willy has a sharp and fresh vision and that wonderful gift which is typical of great French writers, for describing a thing in a few decisive lines, for discovering the right and sometimes unexpected adjective, for pointing out the one essential and exceptional detail in a character —where lesser writers would write pages of dull, obvious and almost meaningless disquisitions.

But *L'Envers du Music-Hall* does not only possess literary qualities : perfection of form and a sympathetic understanding of certain conditions of life contrive to make this book a most valuable contribution to the literature of the stage.

It is also of theatrical life that M. Charles Henry Hirsch writes in his last novel, and we also find in *Saint-Vallier* (Fasquelle, 3 fr. 50) the same qualities of emotion and pity. *Saint-Vallier* is the lamentable story of a starving old actor who has probably never known better days than those minutely described in these three hundred and fifty pages. He certainly never had talent, but illusions and self-confidence helped him to believe in his genius which, thought he, only bad luck and jealousy have prevented from astonishing Paris. He sees the world through the veil of dramatic literature and to him (until the very end of his miserable days) life is only a pretext for splendid theatrical effects ; yet that is because he is so much in earnest and so full of enthusiasm for his art and his would-be glory.

It is in one of these small provincial towns in which Saint-Vallier once played small parts that is laid the scene of M. Henry Bordeaux's novel. *La Maison* (Plon-Nourrit, 3 fr. 50) belongs to that class of grey, rather dull and indifferently written books which, for some mysterious reason, always seem to reach twenty or thirty editions. Of course, it is clever, but oh ! so aggressively catholic, patriotic (in the narrowest sense of the word) and *bien pensant*. Such people as the heroes of *La Maison* no doubt exist in large quantities, but their story is the rather uninteresting story of many French families, and the *banalités* of life are apt to become tedious unless treated by a Balzac, a Flaubert or an Anatole France. The characters of M. Henry Bordeaux's ambitious book ought to be satisfied with being readers—not heroes—of novels.

Les Noces Folles (Bernard Grasset, 3fr. 50) is a love story pure and simple, in which M. Eugène Montfort shows us first the wonderful love affair, then the conflict between an Italian woman and her Parisian husband. All that seemed in her divinely beautiful against a background of romantic Napolitan scenery soon becomes out of place in modern Paris. He falls in love with another woman only to discover later—too late—when after a similar incident his wife leaves him, that his love for her is as passionate as before.

As for *Paroles devant la Vie* (E. Figuière, 3fr. 50) it is a remarkable collection of strange comparisons, far-fetched adjectives, invented words, lyrical sentences and second-hand metaphysical ideas. I take it that M. Alexandre Mercereau is hailed as a genius by many of his friends. It seems to me that he is specially clever at discovering the obvious : he wonders at everything and everybody, Life, Death, Maternity, The Poet, Pantheism, Himself and His New Flat. *Paroles*, indeed, and not much else. His *Paroles devant la nouvelle demeure* afford a typical example of his talent (including a " *sombre étoffe londonienne* " unknown to English decorators, which shows his mania for using at any cost an unexpected epithet). Miss Victoria Monks used to sing a song called " Moving Day " which was, I think, much more to the point.

MUSIC By W. DENIS BROWNE

Wolf-Ferrari, Henschel, Fanelli

ONE of our habits in England is to produce foreign works with a flourish of trumpets a dozen years or so after their first appearance abroad ; by which time their vitality is generally exhausted and their novelty gone. It was really hardly worth Mr. Fagge's while to disinter the " Vita Nuova " for the sake of saying " first performance in England." Wolf-Ferrari is not a great composer, and never will be : he tries to graft German methods on to an Italian temperament, and the result is confusion of style. The " Vita Nuova " is really nothing more than a student work. Regarded as a setting of a poem that is as familiar to most Italians as the Lord's Prayer is to us, it naturally loses much of its effect when sung to a translation : and as it was done the other day all the intimacy of the original vanished. Chorus and orchestra ploughed through it in strict time without any of the rubato that the composer goes out of his way to demand in a note at the beginning of the score. The tendency of the music is naturally towards frequent accelerandos and crescendos ; he has accordingly contented himself with purely negative indications of diminuendo and ritenuto. Mr. Fagge's Procrustean beat however never once allowed the music to play itself, and the naive melodies and simple orchestration, which, treated gently, would have been quite effective, sounded simply stiff and affected.

Another semi-new arrival was Dr. Henschel's Requiem. It was very well performed by the Handel Society. The soloists were admirable and the chorus and orchestra—mainly amateur—quite excellent. I mention the soloists first, because it is of them that Dr. Henschel seems to have thought most when he was writing it. The four solo parts melt into one another with delicious intricacy ; if anything is to be said against the work, perhaps the writing is a little too elaborate and consciously beautiful. The blending is not so noticeable in the chorus-writing ; the joins here are sometimes perceptible and there are gaps just in the places where continuity is most needed. There are besides far too many climaxes of sound : they average about one to a page. But there is a great deal of beauty everywhere, and sincerity too. Dr. Henschel writes strong and musical counterpoint ; he has a vivid sense of tonality and that power that Schubert had of momentarily disturbing harmonies without shifting the key-centre ; above all he has the gift of writing long tunes. He could not, of course, help being influenced by other writers of requiems, but he has kept his own individuality in spite of them. Mozart and Brahms can be traced in his mental attitude towards the text, and Wagner in his musical treatment of it ; but not one of them really obscures his personality in a single bar.

The performance of Fanelli's " Tableaux Symphoniques " by the Colonne Orchestra of Paris was unsuccessful for much the same reason as the " Vita Nuova," except that Fanelli was much more in advance of his period (the eighties) than Wolf-Ferrari is or ever could be in advance of his. M. Pierné's discovery has come too late to do either us or Fanelli any good. There are a number of curious anticipations of modern colour in the three pieces, but they are too shapeless to be effective. There is undeniable atmosphere in them all, particularly in the third piece, the insistence of which becomes almost maddening after a time. Fanelli might have been a great genius if he could have heard his compositions played when he was younger : but years of privation and neglect have let his ideas run to seed and left his technique sprawling.

Among the excitement of all these " discoveries " an unostentatious revival has been quietly going on elsewhere. The Carl Rosa Company have been performing Mozart's " Magic Flute " in English at the Coronet Theatre. It was a modest performance, but none the less interesting for that ; and is likely to do the cause of opera far more real good than sixty Covent Gardens. But I suppose the latter institution will go on thrusting Ricordi operas and rubbish like " Oberst Chabert " down our throats until the Day of Judgment.

THE GALLERIES

Mr. Max Beerbohm's Exhibition

By EDWARD MARSH

MR. BEERBOHM continues to keep us amused. His "Garland" was the principal boon and blessing of last Christmas; and now people are four deep round his little roomful of caricatures, and to see them at all one must take one's place in a queue like a first-nighter at the mouth of the pit.

No one in England, except Rossetti, has reached such mastery in the two arts of pen and pencil; (and even this compliment must be strengthened if we are to believe Mr. Chesterton, who has just told us surprisingly that Rossetti was only successful in both because he was not very good at either). This is the more remarkable because his method of parody and his method of caricature are so distinct. His parodies are written from within. He seems to possess his victims like the imp of some severely logical nightmare, guiding them into strangely familiar surroundings, in which they remain themselves, only more so. He gets into their skins like a refined Sally Beauchamp, and jerks them into odd characteristic attitudes. He is a hypnotist, who shows us his subjects politely and cheerfully drinking methylated spirit in the belief that it is ice-cream-soda. Roughly speaking, no "Max" disengages himself: we have only Messrs. ——, ——, and ——, in their habits as we know them, but a little off the rails. In his caricatures, on the other hand, he is entirely the outside observer and critic. There is far more exaggeration and distortion; and though there is equal subtlety, it is shown rather in choosing a point of departure than in keeping up a perfidiously faithful companionship. And everywhere we are conscious of Max—a grave, ironic, penetrating, Olympian sprite.

The exaggeration and distortion are now less pronounced than they were in much of his earlier work. His figures might still be described in the words of Mr. Rupert Brooke:

> "Straggling, irregular, perplexed, embossed,
> Grotesquely twined, extravagantly lost

By crescive paths and strange protuberant ways
From sanity and from wholeness and from grace."

But he seems to be gradually abandoning the almost purely " constructive designs " of which the " Lord Burnham " and the " Mr. Teixeira de Mattos " are the chief examples here. Perhaps he is leaving them to the Futurists ; but, for whatever reason, his personages are steadily becoming more human. This is of advantage to his work in one of its aspects. There can be no doubt that he will be among the chief sources for the intellectual and political history of our time. Perhaps, by the way, he is also one of its makers ; it is difficult to suppose that No. 16 will not be " another nail in the coffin of Tariff Reform," or that after seeing No. 3 Mr. Arnold Bennett will not be shamed into finishing the *Clayhanger* series. But be that as it may, it is to be hoped that when Mr. Beerbohm's work is completed, it will be made the foundation of an " Illustrated History of England " for his period, which then —thanks to his unfailing eye for the centre of a situation, and his gift for fixing it in a memorably comic form—will live with incomparable vividness in the minds of a delighted posterity.

From this point of view it is a misfortune that among so many brilliant successes he has a certain number of notable failures in likeness. Lord Curzon, for instance, Lord Milner, Mr. Anthony Hope, Mr. Albert Rothenstein, and Sir Edgar Speyer, are surely almost unrecognisable. A plea may be put in for the Prime Minister's nose ; Mr. Lloyd George seems to have got mixed up with Mr. Keir Hardie ; and, worst of all, Sir Edward Grey, in the embrace of the Russian bear, suggests rather Mr. Donald Tovey struggling to escape from the influence of Stravinsky.

But what are these among so many ? and even if there were fewer successes with individuals to set against them, there would remain the types. Here are three groups which are miracles of various invention at work on the results of observation : the Colonels at the Cavalry Club, the Dons at Magdalen, and the Labour Members fascinated by Lord Alexander Thynne ; and the group of great ladies listening to Mr. Percy Grainger, though less individualised, is an equally wonderful *ensemble*. Mr. Beerbohm's vision of the eighteenth, nineteenth and twentieth centuries is a more transcendental example of his fine historic sense.

He has among his invaluable qualifications for this *rôle* of historian a sense of proportion and an instinct for greatness. He may be occasionally unkind to mediocrities ; but never in his wildest farce does he fail to pay some tribute, however mixed, to a big quality in a man. Take the sublime absurdity of his Mr. Balfour, clasping the " curves of his gradual violin " while he elegantly applauds Mr. Bonar Law dinning on the big drum. Take the tortuous, warped power of his " Lord Hugh Cecil." Take the " Gabriele d'Annunzio," with the fire of genius and poetry smouldering through the sensual vulgarity of the *rastaquouère*. Perhaps the finest example is the " Mr. John Masefield," towering like Gulliver, in his fastidious melancholy sympathy, over the roofs of the slum, from the lips of whose denizens he is so gravely noting down swear-words for future use. This is Mr. Beerbohm's strength as an apologist (conscious or unconscious), that in the act of giving his man away with both hands, making every point against him, and surrendering all his weak places to the Comic Spirit, he yet leaves him a great creature.

His technical equipment is a curious mixture. There is, of course, a negligible sense in which he is no draughtsman. He does not, perhaps cannot, and probably does not care to make his figures stand on their feet or sit in their chairs ; yet he is a master of expressive line. Sometimes his composition seems haphazard : sometimes every touch falls into its place in a monumental design. Sometimes his colour is neither here nor there ; but occasionally, as in the buffs and crimsons of the " Count Boni de Castellane " it flowers into such a harmony that one almost overlooks the comic quality of the drawing.

A word must be said of the perfect style of his titles and legends —the little imperishable niggles at the bottom of the pictures.

" Amurath and Amurazzle," for Mr. Balfour and Mr. Bonar Law, is perhaps the wittiest where all are witty. But wherever there is a tone to be caught, Mr. Beerbohm catches it and fixes it in a sentence ; as in the words from a Nobleman's Memoirs, which the Industrious Anonyma, a gaunt bespectacled spinster, is dictating, in the most purely and deliciously ludicrous of the drawings, to a slightly bewildered typist : " *I saw a good lot of the Prince of Wales —afterwards Edward VII.—in those days, and I must say that a better sportsman—and, I may add, a better pal—never stepped in shoe-leather. I remember once after I had been having rather a rotten day at Newmarket he came up to me and, slapping me on the back, said, etc., etc.*"

Indépendants and the Cubist Muddle By O. RAYMOND DREY

THIS year's Salon des Indépendants, in so far as it counts at all, is a " Cubist " Salon. In an exhibition which stretches nearly to the horizon, where anyone may send his pictures without fear of rejection, for there is no jury, and where apparently everyone does, the critic may reasonably hope to meet with adventures. Somewhere amid the jostle of fashionable, glossy efficiency and crude or glossy incompetence he may light haphazard on a lure beckoning to unknown delights. Somewhere in the ruck may be the choice encounter of a lifetime.

For lack of such rare stimulus (perhaps my persistence in the teeming rooms was not equal to my opportunity) I am forced to the consideration of the word " Cubism." It is a slushy term enough as it is used to-day. Probably it was never very finely intentioned. The public clamours for a name, and painters or writers think they have to find one. This labelling is always the price that artists have to pay for recognition, whether they seek it or not. The public likes a school because it finds certainty in numbers ; there is no comfort in the lonely man who paints without a name.

Indépendants and the Cubist Muddle

It is all very well to call certain painters " Cubists " if you are content not to think any more about them after you have agreed on the title. Of course the majority of cultivated people who walk out of picture galleries to talk about art *are* quite content. Simpler people, on the other hand, who walk into picture galleries to enjoy the sight of pictures are either driven away abashed by the name they know they cannot understand, worried into hostility to the artists, or set humbly to the solving of insoluble riddles.

When a number of painters were labelled " Impressionists " less harm was done. " Impressionism " is an abstract term : it is tolerably elastic. The " Glasgow School " had some connection with Glasgow. " Pre-Raphaelitism," silly term though it was, certainly implied reaction. And " Post-Impressionism," with a little licence, is a matter of dates ; whoever chooses may think so, at any rate.

But what does this title " Cubism " mean, which we hear applied so indiscriminately alike to Picasso or Braque and Le Fauconnier ; to Metzinger or Gleizes and to Delaunay (" Orphist" will not stick to him long) ; to Marchand or de la Fresnaye and to L'Hote ; to Picart-LeDoux and to Herbin ? I might add more contrasting names to my list, but there is no need.

Are we to say that a " Cubist " is a man who paints in cubes ? A technical similarity in the means used by all these men at one time or another to express the volume of objects by outlining their planes is a poor excuse for a frivolously superficial definition. When the question is asked what these painters are expressing or trying to express it will be found that no general designation will fit them all ; that if definitions or titles are wanted the painters will have to be taken separately or in groups of twos and threes, with a title for each individual or little group. Such refinement of definition would only make confusion worse confounded.

But rigid definition apart, some sort of philosophic division is necessary if " Cubist " work is to be understood at all. I would consider all the " Cubist " exhibitors in the Indépendants in relation to Picasso, who has no pictures in the Salon, but who is, to my mind, the one man who, sacrificing all thought of representation, of actuality, has achieved a real intensity of expression and found a new way to our emotions, to our capacity for response. One's personal relation to a picture is, after all, the only standard of criticism that has any value. In other words, there are as many standards of criticism as there are critics.

Picasso, then, has come from contemplation of form and substance to an abstract rhythmic statement that is new in paint but old in music. Rhythmic statement is not new in paint. Rhythmic statement independent of concrete representation, abstract rhythmic statement, is. The difficulty that most people find with Picasso is due to this: that never before has painting appealed directly to the emotions without enlisting the aid of the intellect. People complain when music becomes representative, realistic. It is no longer music, we are told. Yet who can say what music is, or what is painting? It is a poor game to try to confine the human spirit, to temper creation, to put our own blinkers on the visionary.

The " Cubists " in the Salon des Indépendants are all, by various means, concerned with seizing and interpreting actuality: space, the play of light on surfaces, the interplay of colour, significant movement. Their failure or success depends both on the measure of intensity with which they are able to invest the new and arbitrary life on their canvasses, and on the quality of that intensity. In the work of M. Gleizes and M. Metzinger, well patterned though it is, I cannot perceive that life has become a fuller thing through paint. M. Delaunay's big picture " L'Equipe de Cardiff F.C." embodies everything which I have credited these " Cubists " with seeking. It is intense, but the intensity is that of Severini's " Café Monico." It is perfectly realistic, flooded with light and air and dancing with movement. The photograph is the lowest denominator of human vision. M. Delaunay seems to have perfected the camera. Well, it takes a clever man to do that!

Volume I Number III JULY 1913 One Shilling Net

THE BLUE REVIEW

LITERATURE DRAMA ART MUSIC

CONTENTS

Poetry Rupert Brooke, W. H. Davies, Iolo Aneurin Williams
Sister Barbara — Gilbert Cannan
Daibutsu — Yone Noguchi
Mr. Bennett, Stendhal and the Modern Novel — John Middleton Murry
Ariadne in Naxos — Edward J. Dent
Epilogue III : Bains Turcs — Katherine Mansfield

CHRONICLES OF THE MONTH

The Theatre (Masefield and Marie Lloyd), Gilbert Cannan ; *The Novels* (Security and Adventure), Hugh Walpole ; *General Literature* (Irish Plays and Playwrights), Frank Swinnerton ; *German Books* (Thomas Mann), D. H. Lawrence ; *Italian Books*, Sydney Waterlow ; *Music* (Elgar, Beethoven, Debussy), W. Denis Browne ; *The Galleries* (Gino Severini), O. Raymond Drey.

MARTIN SECKER PUBLISHER
NUMBER FIVE JOHN STREET ADELPHI

The Imprint

June 17th, 1913

REPRODUCTIONS IN PHOTOGRAVURE
PIONEERS OF PHOTOGRAVURE: By DONALD CAMERON-SWAN, F.R.P.S.
PLEA FOR REFORM OF PRINTING: By TYPOCLASTES
OLD BOOKS & THEIR PRINTERS: By J. ARTHUR HILL
EDWARD ARBER, F.S.A.: By T. EDWARDS JONES
THE PLAIN DEALER: VI. By EVERARD MEYNELL
DECORATION & ITS USES: VI. By EDWARD JOHNSTON
THE BOOK PRETENTIOUS AND OTHER REVIEWS: By J. H. MASON
THE HODGMAN PRESS: By DANIEL T. POWELL
PRINTING & PATENTS: By GEO. H. RAYNER, R.P.A.
PRINTERS' DEVICES: By the Rev. T. F. DIBDIN. PART VI.
REVIEWS, NOTES AND CORRESPONDENCE.

Price One Shilling net

Offices: 11 Henrietta Street, Covent Garden, W.C.

JULY

CONTENTS

		Page
Post Georgian	By X. Marcel Boulestin	*Frontispiece*
Love	By Rupert Brooke	149
The Busy Heart	By Rupert Brooke	150
Love's Youth	By W. H. Davies	151
When We are Old, are Old	By Iolo Aneurin Williams	152
Sister Barbara	By Gilbert Cannan	153
Daibutsu	By Yone Noguchi	160
Mr. Bennett, Stendhal and the Modern Novel	By John Middleton Murry	164
Ariadne in Naxos	By Edward J. Dent	175
Epilogue : III. Bains Turcs	By Katherine Mansfield	181

CHRONICLES OF THE MONTH

The Theatre : Masefield and Marie Lloyd	By Gilbert Cannan	186
The Novels : Security and Adventure	By Hugh Walpole	189
General Literature : Irish Plays and Playwrights	By Frank Swinnerton	194
German Books : Thomas Mann	By D. H. Lawrence	200
Italian Books	By Sydney Waterlow	207
The Galleries : Gino Severini	By O. Raymond Drey	213
Music : Beethoven, Elgar, Debussy	By W. Denis Browne	215

Editor : John Middleton Murry
Associate Editor : Katherine Mansfield
Editorial Office : 57 Chancery Lane, W.C.
Telephone 2132 Holborn

" Post Georgian " By X. Marcel Boulestin

LOVE

Love is a breach in the walls, a broken gate,
  Where that comes in that shall not go again ;
Love sells the proud heart's citadel to Fate.
  They have known shame, who love unloved. Even then,
When two mouths, thirsty each for each, find slaking,
  And agony's forgot, and hushed the crying
Of credulous hearts, in heaven—such are but taking
  Their own poor dreams within their arms, and lying
Each in his lonely night, each with a ghost.
  Some share that night. But they know love grows colder,
Grows false and dull, that was sweet lies at most.
  Astonishment is no more in hand or shoulder,
But darkens, and dies out from kiss to kiss.
All this is love ; and all love is but this.

RUPERT BROOKE.

THE BUSY HEART

Now that we've done our best and worst, and parted,
  I would fill my mind with thoughts that will not rend.
(O heart, I do not dare go empty-hearted)
  I'll think of Love in books, Love without end ;
Women with child, content ; and old men sleeping ;
  And wet strong ploughlands, scarred for certain grain ;
And babes that weep, and so forget their weeping ;
  And the young heavens, forgetful after rain ;
And evening hush, broken by homing wings ;
  And Song's nobility, and Wisdom holy,
That live, we dead. I would think of a thousand things,
  Lovely and durable, and taste them slowly,
One after one, like tasting a sweet food.
I have need to busy my heart with quietude.

RUPERT BROOKE.

LOVE'S YOUTH

Not only is my love a flower
  That blooms in broad daylight,
But, like the Evening Primrose, it
  Will bloom again at night.

Though I this day have reached my prime,
  My heart's still fresh and young ;
I tremble at young Beauty's glance,
  And love is still my song.

At thy bright smile I burn and shake,
  Though treated as thy brother ;
Canst thou not see my eyes have twins
  That laugh and call thee mother ?

WILLIAM H. DAVIES.

WHEN WE ARE OLD, ARE OLD

Age is a large, untidy hall
  With a little fire and a draughty door,
Where the great beginnings of nothing-at-all
  Hobnob on the littered floor.

And they chatter over the rags, the old,
  With " This was a flaming kiss,"
Or, " Men would dream were this thing told,
  And men would weep were this."

And thither shall you and I come, too,
  And walk in the chilly place ;
And I shall still be praising you,
  Though the young men laugh in my face.

And the broken words of the once sweet tongue
  Shall feel about in the gloom,
And echoes of all that we said when young
  Go racketting round the room.

IOLO ANEURIN WILLIAMS.

SISTER BARBARA
By GILBERT CANNAN

GENERAL BRIERLEY had very definite ideas as to how a gentleman should live, and in the realisation of them had surrounded himself with many possessions, two houses, a wife, two daughters and a son who should follow in his footsteps. When he retired and found his income reduced by two-thirds, he clung to all his possessions, for without them he felt that he could not maintain his position as a gentleman. His son married early and wisely and, when his father looked to him for assistance in those difficulties which beset a gentleman, quarrelled with him, transferred himself to another regiment and went to India. Of the two daughters, one was pretty and attractive to men, and to her whims and desires the other, Barbara, was sacrificed. When the General's difficulties grew to such proportions that he had to rid himself of one of his possessions, he decided that Barbara must go out into the world to earn her living. She had had only the most foolish kind of education and possessed no craft nor art nor marketable accomplishment. Further, she was a lady and therefore cut off from the practice of many trades. She was very religious and solved the problem by returning to a girlish aspiration and becoming a nun. She thought no ill of her father, who protested his affection and bemoaned their harsh necessity. He took her to the station and paid for her third-class ticket.

II

She was in the convent for eleven years. In the beginning she found it a little difficult to fall in with the monotonous routine of the place and to overcome her repulsion from the rough domestic labours which she had to undertake. She learned to cook and sew and darn and mend and clean, and when she was entrusted with the care of the children her education began. Her refinement and sensitiveness made her successful with them and little by little the Mother Superior promoted her to full control of that part of the convent's activity. She was so absorbed and busy that she had little time for thought of the outside world and she rarely communicated with her family. She heard that her sister was married —" a splendid position "—and wrote to congratulate her. Then she did not write again for years. She was neither very happy nor very unhappy : her busy life left no room for violent variations of moral temperature and she was puzzled and distressed by the emotional fervour which some of the sisters brought to the practice of their religion.

The convent belonged to a world-wide sisterhood, and twice the Mother Superior sent Sister Barbara over to houses in France and Belgium. She displayed excellent tact and business capacity and the supreme authority marked her out for diplomatic missions. Far rather would she have stayed with her children, but obedience was an element in her vow and she obeyed. She was sent to New York, to South Africa, to Manila, and she saw the activity of the outside world and was excited by it. She counted her excitement for a sin and her conscience scourged her, but it was not long before she saw that the business organisation of the sisterhood was neither better nor worse than other commercial undertakings, and therefore in flat contradiction to the principles of religion. In the simplicity and directness of her nature she hated to have her life broken up into two portions, between profession and practice.

When she consulted the Mother Superior on her scruples, she was told that the Mother Church must be maintained and had to fight for her existence : was she not the Church Militant ? Sister Barbara procured a promise that she should not be sent abroad again for some time, and she returned to her children. Then, however, she found herself thinking of them in a new way. Not as little units in the Church, but as individuals, who would grow up and go out into the warm, bright, multi-coloured movement of the world. It was that, or the pure white radiance of the cloistered life. But the cloistered life, as she could not but admit to herself, was neither pure nor white.

A girl who had come to the convent to hide away from her grief and shame in an unhappy love-affair, confided in her, told all the story of her love. She did not tell the truth and it was not a beautiful story, but there was warmth in it and a tiny spasm of passion. It filled Sister Barbara's thoughts and she was very unhappy. She found herself going over the eleven years, wiping them out as though they had never been and living again in her father's house. If she had stayed . . . If she had stayed ? . . .

She told the Mother Superior that she must return. There was no room for argument : she must return to the world.

III

She found no welcome. Nothing had changed in her home. Still her father was spending twice his income. Still her mother was ruled by her sister, who had left her husband and taken up her old position at home, filling the house with men, young and old, seeking pleasure at every turn. She found no welcome. They were in the midst of a financial crisis and by way of retrenchment had dismissed two of their servants. The cook demanded more wages and was dismissed. Barbara undertook the cooking and the housekeeping. The waste, the extravagance offended her, and she could not but try to reform the household. The greatest leakage was through her sister, who always seemed to have money for her every whim. Where before she was indulged on the prospect of a successful marriage, now she was humoured on the score of her conjugal failure. She was still spoiled and pretty and there was no alteration in her character or her conduct. Barbara found her father every day more pompously querulous, her mother more foolish, her sister self-willed and thoughtless. Accustomed as she was to the acute economy of the convent, the thriftlessness of this household appalled her and she could not see how a catastrophe had been averted. Her father did not know either, but he supposed that the danger would be avoided as others had been avoided before. Certain reforms Barbara was able to accomplish. On the strength of them her father bought a motor-car, which her sister monopolised.

More even than her changes, Barbara's family resented her competence and thoroughness. A storm gathered, grew, broke and Barbara's mother declared that one or other of the sisters must leave the house. It was Barbara who went, and she took a room in a cheap Bloomsbury boarding-house, her father making her an allowance of one pound a week until she should be in a position to maintain herself. She set herself to learn type-writing and shorthand, and often she told herself that it had been folly to leave the convent, that life in the world was impossible and mean and dull. Her co-inhabitants in the boarding-house were all in as poor a plight as she, and they were shy and awkward with each other or took refuge in the traditional humour of the place.

When she had mastered her new work she was faced with the impossibility of finding a situation. Always the youth or prettiness of her competitors thrust her into the background. She took herself in hand, watched other women for the tricks she had forgotten or never acquired, recollected her sister's ways for the details and subtle refinements which had gone to the making of her charm. She imitated these things but despised them because they were not part of herself. Her luck did not turn and she began to think that something of the nunnery must cling about her. She was too vigorous to feel that her age might be a handicap.

In four months she had not earned a penny and her family seemed completely to have forgotten her, except that once her sister drove up in the motor-car and left her a parcel of clothes that "might be useful to her." She saw the car as she was coming wearily home in the afternoon and waited until her sister had gone.

Three days later she had the excitement of finding a letter on her plate at breakfast. The other boarders eyed her as she opened it. She felt them watching her and gave no sign, folded it up and laid it on the table. It was short, and a bare statement from her mother that her father was so straitened for money that it would be impossible to continue her allowance. . . . In her purse she had five shillings and threepence halfpenny. She gulped down her breakfast and one by one the other boarders went away until she was left alone except for the quiet man with the brown eyes who always sat at the other end of the table. With her eyes staring in front of her she sat and she felt hard and withered. It was the tone of her mother's letter that had hurt her so, that she could hardly realise its contents.

The quiet man came towards her, stood by her side and said :

" We seem to be in the same boat. I should like to be able to help you."

She resented his intrusion but she could make no reply. Even an impertinence was something to fill the emptiness about and within her. He went on :

" You can't talk about trouble straight off. At least, I can't. Will you dine with me to-night at the Tellier in Soho ? You can get a very good dinner there for a shilling."

She looked up at him and there was a twinkle in his eyes and much friendliness. A shilling dinner seemed a good joke and instinctively they agreed to laugh at it together, and so use it to brush aside awkwardness and embarrassment and the savage egoism of loneliness.

Yes. She would dine with him that night at seven.

" I, too," he said, " am going to look for work."

That also was a joke and it appealed to her as a humorous coincidence that another creature should spend the day in looking for work.

The day passed quickly and she was punctual, to find him waiting for her at the Tellier.

" Any luck ? " he said.

" No."

" Neither had I. How much money have you got ?' '

" Five shillings."

" I have fourteen and sixpence. We'd better pool it and then it will go farther for both of us."

She agreed and he said :

" Now I'll tell you my story. I was married until a year ago. I was in business in Leicestershire and we had a fine house, land, horses, people we called friends and all that. I'd been married eight years. For various reasons, the most fundamental of which were probably physical and therefore impossible for my wife to face, we drifted apart, so far that we shared nothing but the habit of marriage. That was deadly. My wife couldn't or wouldn't see it and was outraged when I suggested a separation. She didn't want to lose her position. She cared about the people we called friends and the money and the house, and as I couldn't make her see the reason for throwing it all up and trying another arrangement, in a fit of desperation I said she could keep all that if she'd only let me go. She couldn't see why I wanted to go, but she did feel that to keep me might be dangerous, so she agreed to that. I kept my word. I took just enough to keep me for a year, for I had an idea the best thing for me was to make my own way and not to go on living padded in with stocks and shares in other people's work. I cut away pretty thoroughly, perhaps too thoroughly. Anyhow, here I am. I haven't got any work. I shan't be able to pay my rent, but I'd rather sleep on the Embankment than appeal to anyone for money. The only thing I miss is the horses. I walk in the Park sometimes and hate the people who have got them."

She told her story.

" The only thing I miss is the children. I was always learning from them. You know, growing."

" I know."

He took her hand in his.

That night they walked miles through the streets of London.

She was the first to procure work at thirty shillings a week, and with the confidence this gave her she pocketed her pride and worried her father's distinguished and busy friends until they gave her extra work in the evenings. Upon that she took three rooms in a shabby district, high up with a view of Hampstead from her windows. She saw her friend every day. Every night they dined together and very soon, through her, he too obtained a situation. They pooled all their earnings and it was at her suggestion that he came to lodge in her rooms.

For long they hovered in the outer dreamland of unspoken love, but love was theirs and would not be denied. Out of their misery grew wonders and they were born again, his old life and hers lost in the new life they had together builded.

Often they walk together in the park and gaze at the horses, and every penny they can save is put by for the purchase of a little house in the country where they can keep a horse and trap. That is all his desire and with his happiness she will be content.

DAIBUTSU By YONE NOGUCHI

THE valley, a snug basin forgotten by consciousness, was filled with the autumnal sunlight of gold, which shone up to the tremendous face of Daibutsu (famous holiness at Kamakura) who, like thought touched by emotion, appeared as if vibrating; Nature there was in the last stage of all evolution, having her energy and strength vaporised into repose. The trees, flowers and grasses in the sacred ground calmed down, to speak somewhat hyperbolically, into the state of Nirvana. The thought that I was a sea-tossed boat even with all oars broken, formed itself then in my mind; it was natural I felt at once that it was the only place, at least in Japan, where my sea-wounded heart would soon be healed by the virtue of my own prayer, and by the air mist-purple filling the valley most voluptuously. I cannot forget my impression when I heard there the evening bell ring out and the voice of sutra-reading from the temple, and how I lost my human thirst and pride, becoming a faint soul, a streak of scent or a wisp of sigh; I was a song itself which grew out from my confession. Such was my first impression on finding myself in Daibutsu's ground, the haven of peace and heavenly love all by itself, soon after I returned home from my long foreign sojourn, that is quite many years ago now; but it seems it was only yesterday that I, like a thousand waves hurrying toward the Yuigahana shore of Kamakura, hurried to Daibutsu with my own soul of wave-like song of prayer; can our human souls ever be more than the waves of the sea?

It was the next summer that I had many many more occasions to lay my body and soul under the blessing of Daibutsu's valley (Oh, what a scent that is the Lord Buddha's!) as I had many weeks to spend there at Kamakura: Summer, the month of my love, with the burning ecstasy that would soon be intensified into the greyness of Oriental desolation. I like the Summer heat, you understand, not from the fact of heat itself, but from the reason we have to thank its presence for the sweetening of the shadows of trees, where I will build, while looking at the delicious white feet of passing breezes, my own kingdom with sighing ; to speak plainly, dream old Kamakura of the Middle Age, that is, of art and religious faith. To-day, it is in truth a common sort of country town of modern Japan, of stereotyped pattern with others ; if there is a difference, it is only in its appearing less individual and far sadder because it has had such a great history, when we observe that its general ambition now points toward commercialism. But it is during those summer weeks only that we can fairly well connect it with the old art and prayer, let me say, with the true existence of Daibutsu the wonder, as we see then with our living eyes the thousand pilgrims in white cotton, bamboo mushroom hats on head and holy staff in hand, and sacred little bells around their waists (what desolate voices of bells !) swarming here mainly to kneel before Daibutsu from every corner of the country where all winds come from ; I was glad to see the whole town religiously changed at once. How often I found myself with those pilgrims, muttering the holy words in Daibutsu's valley, where the nature, not unlike that of the former October of rest, was in all its spiritual ascetiscism with repentance and belief ; the gigantic divinity in bronze, of folded hands and inclined head in heavenly meditation, over whom time and change (summer heat, of course) have no power to stir its silence, is self-denial itself. Oh, let my heart burn in storm and confession like the hearts of a thousand cicadas whose songs almost shake the valley and trees ; we might get the spiritual ascendency out of physical exhaustion ; it makes at least one step nearer our salvation. The autumnal rest or silence can only be gained after having all the summer heart-cry ; isn't Daibutsu's self-denial the heart-cry strengthened into silence ?

There is in this statue a great subtlety, speaking of it as a creation of art, which might result, let me define it arbitrarily, from a good balance of the masses of idealism and what we generally understand as realism ; as the latter is indeed so slight, even our modern imagination whose rush is always proved to be disturbing, has enough room here to play to its content. The proof that the said idealism and realism melt into one another in such a perfection is clearly seen in its external monotony, or, let me say, in its utter sacrifice of gross effect ; while it, on the other hand, has gained the inward richness most magically. To call it an accident is not quite satisfactory, although I do not know how far it is explained by saying that it is the realisation of magic or power of prayer which our ancestors placed in bronze ; there is no denying, I think, that it is the work of prayer to a great measure. Tradition says :

It was Itano no Tsubone, one of the waiting ladies to Shogun Yoritomo, who undertook, when he passed away with unfulfilled desire to have an object of worship at Kamakura, his own capital, similar to the Daibutsu at Nara, to collect a general contribution and fund, with the assistance of the priest Joko ; the first image which was of wood was finished in 1238 or the first year of Rekinin. She was again called to action, when in the autumn of the second year of Hoji (1248) the image, also the chapel, was overthrown by a storm, this time assisted by the Shogun Prince Munetaka, and successfully restored the image in bronze. The artist who executed it was Goroyemon Ono of Yanamura of the Kadzusa province.

Putting aside the question who was Ono and Itano no Tsubone, the significant point is that it was created by a thousand people whose religious longing and hope were fulfilled in this Daibutsu. It is not our imagination alone to think that the statue lives as it is the real force of prayer ; when we see it, we build the most musical relation one with another at once, because we forget ourselves in one soul and body, we might say, in one sound and one colour, perfectly wedded with it. After all, it is nothing but our own emotion and yearning personified.

I believe that it might not have been so great an art as it is if it had been made in our day, mainly because it would express too delicate details ; and the temple light from the opening of the doors, when it used to stand within, must have often played with it unjustly. But it became a great art when the storm and tidal waves destroyed the temple and washed the statue in 1355 and again in 1526, and left it without ever since, with the rustling trees behind, the light and winds crawling up and down, against whose undecidedness its eternal silence would be doubly forcible. Is it not that our human souls often grow beautiful under the baptism of misfortune and grief ? So Nature once unkind to the statue proves to be a blessing to-day ; it looms with far greater divinity out of the rain, wind, lights of sun and moon, whose subtle contribution it fully acknowledges. Where are the foolish people who wish to build the temple again to put the image in ?

MR. BENNETT, STENDHAL AND THE MODERN NOVEL

By JOHN MIDDLETON MURRY

IT may easily seem impertinent for one who has no claim to the title of novelist, whose writings in all would make only a slender book, to criticise an article upon " Writing Novels " by Mr. Arnold Bennett, who might with reason claim to be a representative English novelist, whose writings are encyclopædic in volume and variety. It may seem particularly impertinent, when, as is actually the case, the article in question is among the best of the multifarious deliverances of the author upon the science and practice of the writer's craft. It is, however, exactly this extremity of impertinence which is in itself the justification of the critical attitude in a writer of the younger generation; for if the younger generation (for which, even though it be probably non-existent, I am the self-constituted spokesman) has ideas or principles to put forward which are to govern its own attitude towards such an important literary question as the essentials of the great novel, no better occasion could be found than the presentation by one of the most accomplished novelists of the present day of his own matured conceptions of the subject. In brief, I wish to use Mr. Arnold Bennett's article as a *point d'appui* for my own considerations upon the novel, not as an object of critical attack.

" J'appartiens," as Charles Louis Philippe wrote to Barrès in 1903, " à une génération qui n'a pas encore passé par les livres " ; and for this reason though my ideas can have but little authority, I am in equally little danger of finding my theory confronted and shattered by my practice.

With Mr. Arnold Bennett's obiter dicta I have but little concern. They are generally illuminating; and they are evidence of a breadth of reading which must be rare among modern novelists in England, if we may judge by their production. There are, however, two statements in the article which touch the very vitals of the modern conception of narrative fiction, and these must be examined; for it is probable that in the analysis may be found some reason for the conviction that modern English novelists are on the wrong track.

There is the simple flavour of an axiom in the assertion that " The novelist is he who has seen life and is so excited by it that he absolutely must transmit the vision to others. . . . Only he differs from most artists in this, that what most chiefly strikes him is the indefinable humanness of human nature, the large general manner of existing." The fundamental of the great novelist is " to have an impassioned vision of life." It is so concise and so vague that it seems to be self-evident. It is hardly fruitful. To feel passionately about life is characteristic of a great many people other than novelists. The philosopher, the politician, above all, the social reformer, feel very passionately about life. The feeling is certainly the very germ of the social reformer's activity, and in order to feed the flame of his passionate feeling, he finds it necessary to comprehend more and more of the whole of life, by using algebraical symbols for its constituent parts.

Not only does the social reformer's passionate feeling about life burst through the fetters he has imposed upon himself by his unit-treatment of individuals, but this very process is essential to prolong and intensify his passion. By it he includes infinitely more in his vision. Yet no one would for a moment doubt that the comprehensive passion of the social reformer is something which differs not only in degree, but in kind, from the consciousness of the novelist. Life is a simple word, and a very big word ; and it is easy to convince yourself that you have said something very profound when you have made a simple assertion about life. Just as we object to one novelist who tells us " Life is all very jolly, if you only knew," that he doesn't know very much about it ; so we object when another novelist tells us that the essential to a great novel is a passionate vision of life. It is so vague that it is meaningless ; if it means anything, the expression of that meaning is to be sought in social propaganda, and not in the novel.

The great novelist is passionately interested in individuals.

Take the three who are, in my opinion, the greatest, Stendhal, Tolstoy, and Dostoievsky. They are remembered by their creation of great individual characters, Sanseverina, Anna Karenin, Raskolnikoff; and it is characteristic of such created individuals that they cannot be recognised in " real life." I never hope to meet a Sanseverina, a Comte de Mosca, or a Mlle. de la Mole. However limited in its field were my passionate feeling about life I should never find any individuals who represented in themselves so completely the highest possibilities of humanity. Their supreme individuality is the novelist's creation, coming from the novelist's own brain, in a certain vague sense the " objectification " of his own personality. The work of the great novelist consists in the creation of such characters, not in recognising them in life, for they cannot be recognised, and even if it were by a miracle possible, the artist could never " get inside " them and retain his power of conscious analysis in the very act of their willing and feeling. Yet these characters are the end and justification of the novelist; in them we acknowledge the greatness of the great novelist.

In creating one of these supreme individuals the novelist seems to reveal something of the human soul, and the essence of revelation is to tell us something that we did not know before. The point at which we begin to appreciate the creation is the point at which our own knowledge of the human soul is exhausted. We follow the hero to a crisis in tense intellectual and emotional excitement and we are nonplussed, knowing nothing of how he will act, how he will feel or develop. We could, were we in the frame of mind, suggest alternative lines of action, yet none is inevitable; the logic which we obey is the logic of the type, and we are dealing with an individual. The great novelist takes a line of action or of feeling, either among the alternatives we ourselves might have imagined or something completely outside our reckoning; and from the very moment it is chosen we see its inevitability. We recognise the good logic, which, as Stendhal says, is at the bottom of every genius. Looking back in the newly created light we can see wherein the character possessed real individuality, wherein he differed from the type to which we momentarily assimilated him. In the individuality of the character lies its humanity, not in its approximation to type; and the creation of an individual character is a revelation of humanity, an addition to the knowledge of the human heart.

If it is possible in any degree to discover the conditions of this revelation we may be reasonably certain that in them is to be found something essential to the greatest achievement in narrative fiction. Accepting as we do, though in a restricted sense, that the revelation must be in the last resort the author's revelation of himself, the novelist must be what Taine called Stendhal, *un esprit supérieur*. If he is to follow the analysis of the finest sentiments and emotions of the finest individuals beyond what we already know to a point at which we are dazzled by the illumination suddenly cast upon a human mind, then he must be of this fine mould himself, with an infinite capacity for analysing his own consciousness with definiteness and lucidity. There is a hint of snobbishness in the term *esprit supérieur ;* but the snobbishness corresponds to a reality, for a capacity for self-analysis is the accompaniment of the conviction that the self is fine and important. Aristocracy of the intellect is inevitable in a great novelist. " J'ai horreur du bas peuple," says Stendhal in one form or another throughout his Journal and his autobiography; but Stendhal is not horrified because the proletariat is dirty and does not foregather in salons, but because it is " infiniment plat," ineffably dull. The novelist cannot be interested in chrysalis humanity. When Tolstoy abandoned this attitude, he abandoned also the writing of masterpieces. Dostoievsky was aristocratic by reason of his very infirmity; and we know from the opening chapters of the " House of the Dead " how congenial he found the *bas peuple* of Siberia.

Aristocracy of the intellect is no less inevitable in the created character. Apart from the fact that the relation of the creation to the creator is definite it is impossible to reveal the human heart unless a character is chosen which is itself the realisation of some of the finest possibilities of humanity. The power of rational analysis of motive and action, a clear vision of the working of his own mind,—these are the capacities which belong to the fine character. The working of instinct, or rather the unconsciousness that it is instinct which is working, is typical of a lower plane of existence, in which the novelist cannot find the elements of his supreme individuals. For a revelation of the human soul in a character of fiction demands what philosophers call the continuity of the self, and demands that this continuity should be made explicit. Throughout its development the soul must be self-conscious, analysing its motives and feelings, making the psychological evolution plain to us at the same time that we are carried to a point beyond our knowledge and learn more than we knew of the human heart. If instinct breaks into this continuity the hero must be conscious of the fact that it is instinct which breaks in, for to interrupt the evolution of a soul by some unconscious instinctive reaction, would be like interrupting a chain of good mathematical reasoning by the assertion that $2 + 2 = 5$. Once continuity is lost the creation is annihilated. Not a step can be omitted in the *bonne logique au fond de tout génie*. It is plain then that this continuity of consciousness cannot be expressed in any character save one of an " aristocratic " type. It is not an aristocracy of externals (though it is worth remembering that what I consider to be the finest novel ever written, *La Chartreuse de Parme*, is in such a setting), but an aristocracy of soul, and the character must have realised the main elements of this lofty possibility before the action begins. Otherwise whence can the internal lucidity of consciousness, which makes the working of a soul clear, be derived ? We need to see the character *in the very act* of willing and feeling ; and we are grown a little tired of watching our modern novelists urge their undistinguished puppets to an unattainable perfection. Even the half-instinctive gropings of the half-distinguished in divine discontent with the existing social order have lost their fascination for us; and perhaps we were asking a question of a more critical importance than we knew when we asked Mr. Wells and Mr. Bennett where it was all leading to. We were impatient that their characters should realise themselves and begin. So much of modern novel writing amounts to nothing more than a mere skirmish with preliminaries. Sparring is all very well, and helps to make the fighter fit to battle for world's championships; but too much sparring is not only tedious, as habitués of the Wonderland know, but destroys the ability to fight in real earnest. Perhaps our novelists have spent so much time in sparring that they have forgotten, if they ever knew, how to fight.

One of the manifestations of sparring which we deplore in modern novelists is the preoccupation with the lower middle-class *as such*. This preoccupation, never more in evidence than it is at the present, is probably due to two influences — the prevalence of autobiographical fiction, and the fact that the greater part of modern intellectual unrest centres in the middle classes. Autobiographical fiction is not only the result of an entirely false deduction from the constant relation between the writer and the created character, but an evidence of an extraordinary self conceit; for in the first place the fact that a writer is bound to create from his own experience does not, cannot, mean that he merely records the things that he saw and felt in the surroundings and the circumstances in which he actually saw and felt them. After all, the essential of the great novel is *creation*. In the second place, to consider that the order, the circumstances and the time in which his experiences occurred to him bears the mark of the finger of God so manifestly that his reader will be bound to consider his autobiography a creation, is an unwarrantable piece of conceit. As to the intellectual unrest of the middle classes, it is very probably true that the insurgence of individuality against the tradition of the family and the obtaining social order is more active here than elsewhere in society. The problem of the family is certainly more acute in the middle classes. But that is in itself no reason why the gropings of the emergent individual towards the larger life, the helpless shaking of despairing hands before a freedom half-experienced, should be the recurrent theme of the modern novel. At any rate, if we are to be kept in the middle classes, and there is not the slightest reason why we should not be, we have a right to expect that the characters should be the " aristocrats " of their own class, *esprits supérieurs*. Why are we continually presented with the spectacle of human beings wavering between unconsciousness and consciousness, much as though the finest intellectual development of humanity were held to be the psychology of a child of three ? The reason is as difficult to fathom as it is certain that such characters absolutely preclude the achievement of the finest results of which the novel *is* capable. Such a conception of the novel leads nowhere and the stigma of loutishness is printed on the books. They deal with the hobbledehoys of modern society. They are hobbledehoy books. There is a touch of vulgarity inseparable from such characters and such books; and we resent the caricature of humanity even more than the vulgarity. It is time we had passed on to the grown man, developed not in stature nor in status, but in mind, the man of whom a true hero can be made.

It would be useless to deny that the tendency of modern fiction, and that too of a generation later than Mr. Wells and Mr. Bennett, is against me, and it is probable that the question will be raised : " To which generation do you belong, and on whose behalf do you speak ? " I can only reply with the phrase of Ch-Louis Philippe which I have used before. It is a virtue, as I count virtue to-day, not to have written a novel at the age of twenty-three. An age which is so richly endowed as the present with critics prolific in visions of promise is a superheated atmosphere for the nascent novelist. His flowering is sudden and his decay catastrophic ; and though it ill befits a writer of the youngest generation to indulge in unctuous proverbs concerning stony ground, it is certain that the novelists to-day are legion who have lost the opportunity of something which they will never capture through their lack of restraint in production. Seeing that there is a yearly production of over two thousand novels, and that the young novelist is modestly content to acknowledge that he does not as yet write as well as the dozen writers who have arrived, it is so easy for any young man of parts to write a novel better, a great deal better, than the average, that it is almost as certain that he will get a great conceit of himself from the critics, as that the critics will groan in mechanical raptures concerning the permanence of his ephemeral work. It would probably be a great deal more fortunate if the young writer to-day had to face the uncomprehending but sturdy bludgeonings of Jeffreys instead of the sickening eulogy of the newspaper reviewers.

The temptations in the path of the young writer are manifold. Autobiographical fiction saves him the trouble of writing a novel at all; uncritical criticism saves him the trouble of writing a second; for the second is written rather to satisfy the expectations of a publisher, and the exigences of a custom requiring at the writer's hands one novel a year, than to prove to himself that he had any gift or the grit to realise it. Now a third chasm yawns in the path. Mr. Arnold Bennett sings like a siren in *The English Review* his seductively ambiguous music to lure the young generation to its complete destruction. " As the years pass I attach less and less importance to technique in fiction. . . . I begin to think that the great masters of fiction are by the nature of their art ordained to be more or less amateurs. . . . I do not know why it should be so, unless because in the exuberance of their power they are impatient of the exactitudes of systematic study and the mere bother of repeated attempts to arrive at a minor perfection." With the point which Mr. Bennett is anxious to make in these ill-considered words we are in absolute agreement. When we compare the novels of Jane Austen with the masterpieces of Tolstoy, Dostoievsky or Stendhal, we are immediately conscious that there is in *Emma* a compact perfection of form against which *The Brothers Karamazov* or even *La Chartreuse de Parme* seem loose-ended, if not actually clumsy. This is a fact which cannot be disputed, even as the fact that these loose-ended novels are *the* masterpieces of narrative fiction cannot be disputed, and it is necessary for the critic to seek some reason for this loss of form in the novelists to whom we owe the supreme creations. But it is absolutely misleading when Mr. Bennett attributes this to an " amateurishness " inevitable in a master, or " to the great novelists' impatience of the exactitudes of systematic study, or the mere bother of repeated attempts to arrive at a minor perfection." Tolstoy and Stendhal were painstaking craftsmen. I believe, though I have no other than internal evidence, that Dostoievsky was continually striving after perfection of form. Stendhal, we know, after reading the criticism of Balzac that he had no style, re-wrote the whole of *La Chartreuse* in a *style plus Balzacien*, and rejected the result. He was preoccupied with questions of style and form ; and the repeated notes in the margin of the unfinished *Vie de Henri Brulard*, " *pas de style soutenu*," " *style un peu plus soutenu*," to guide him in the revision which he never accomplished, are proof positive that " amateurishness " at least is not to be charged to the masters of the novel. The cause is rather to be sought in the very nature of the subject matter of the great novel.

It has been already urged at considerable length that the novelist is passionately interested in individuals and that his achievement consists in the creation of " superior souls." The creation of an individual demands that he should be presented in his full individuality ; and we know without awaiting the corroboration of the philosophers that this full individuality consists not least in relations with other individuals, and the individuality of these others in their relations with others till the whole structure of society is bound together with the created character. The novelist—herein lies the truth of his passionate feeling about life—detaches a portion of the web of relations which constitute life, because it assumes for him an overwhelming importance, and inevitably in the portion detached there are a certain number of loose ends which, throughout the novel, suggest the relation to a world beyond. If he neatly rounds off every end, gives everyone his entrance and his exit within the compass of the novel itself, the inevitable result seems to be a microcosm, such as Jane Austen's. But the supreme novelist, being among other things a supremely honest man, by the very honesty of the severance, suggests that there is another world closely bound with that he creates, and for all he knows, equally valuable and equally capable of expression. The great novels are loose-ended because absolute truth is incompatible with the smaller perfection. We enjoy the microcosm that Jane Austen gives us, though we realise to the full that she is ultimately to be regarded as second-rate. The pessimistic Turgeniev had perfection of form because perhaps the finest expression of pessimism is to tie all the ends of life together. In his books there is nothing out of perspective, and consequently he never achieves that final creation of character that is in the greatest novels. It is difficult exactly to express this conviction of mine in reading Turgeniev. It may be vaguely conveyed by saying that he is faultless as regards the perspective of the individual work of art, but ignores the perspective of spiritual values which seems to transcend the more academic virtues of craftsmanship. The great novelist practises these virtues so long as they are compatible with spiritual truth.

Discarding, then, Mr. Bennett's insidious suggestion of " amateurishness " as a characteristic of the great novelist, we will complete our viaticum for the youngest generation by including our results in a hard saying. He must be an *esprit supérieur ;* he must create *esprits supérieurs ;* he must strive for perfection of form so long as it is compatible with spiritual truth. These commandments are so little in accord with modern practice that it would seem consummate temerity to press our analysis of the great novel yet further. It is, however, impossible to resist the impulse to define the subject matter of the supreme novel even more closely. I think that such novels must deal with the history of a love-passion ; for that is the passion which intensifies a man's humanity to the uttermost. (The possession of an *esprit supérieur*, being man's highest realisation of himself, is his humanity.) Other passions curtail this humanity to varying degrees, and bring him in one respect or another nearer to the beasts that perish. Thus though Old Goriot's passionate affection for his daughters impresses us, we are repelled at the same moment, considering that he is a monomaniac. Similarly we conceive that a passion for power would dehumanise a man. On the other hand a man's love-passion for a woman brings his consciousness to its highest level and maintains it at that level longest. Moreover, there is always immanent in such a passion a sense of approaching tragedy, for it is by its very nature never wholly secure. But the love-passion of the supreme novel must be that of an *esprit supérieur* for an *esprit supérieur ;* for on a lower level of humanity the passion itself becomes grosser, and lessens rather than intensifies a man's humanity. The love-passions of the hobbledehoy books are not love-passions at all ; they are best described by the misused word Sex, and merit all the vituperation bestowed on that word by the *New Age*, which, however, not seldom has the misfortune to include and condemn the higher with the lower. I do not wish to suggest that the novel should be restricted to the history of a love passion—that is the limited sphere of its highest triumphs—but rather to record my conviction that the great novelist of the future will be like the great novelist of the past, a superior spirit creating superior spirits, striving after perfection of form so long as it is compatible with absolute spiritual truth, and achieving his supreme creation in the history of a love passion. If this were the critical instrument in common use to-day, how many of the first-born would be spared, and how many of the adults held in honour ?

ARIADNE IN NAXOS

By EDWARD J. DENT

ANYONE who has ever attempted to learn a foreign language, anyone who has attained a considerable proficiency in it, knows that the most difficult and elusive chapter of his task is the comprehension of foreign humour. There are, of course, certain things which are comic in any language and perhaps to any temperament. Jokes which are primitive and direct we can all understand, and to an Englishman who knows German pretty well, there is a certain amusement to be derived from such literary humour as the parody in German of some classic German author. But supposing that we are confronted with, say, a German parody of a French or Italian author, the difficulty is horribly complicated. We may be quite familiar with the original French or Italian, we may be fluent German scholars ; but there still remains a new effort to be made, and one that demands a peculiar agility of mind. We have got to realise not only what our French author signifies to us, but what he signifies to the average German mind ; and we often are inclined to feel that not only is the effort irksome, but that it is not worth the trouble of making.

The curious entertainment presented a month ago at His Majesty's Theatre under the title of *Ariadne in Naxos* gives unlimited scope to those who care to try psychological experiments of this kind. *Ariadne in Naxos* is an opera performed by order of M. Jourdain in *Le Bourgeois Gentilhomme*. Before we can understand *Ariadne*, then, we must understand M. Jourdain ; not, however, Molière's M. Jourdain, or what we English people think to be Molière's M. Jourdain, but M. Jourdain as seen by Herr von Hoffmannsthal, and perhaps Herr von Hoffmannsthal's M. Jourdain as seen by Mr. Maugham and Sir Herbert Tree.

Fortunately, however, this is not really the case. It is quite evident that this so-called " M. Jourdain " is a man of straw. What the author and composer wanted was an " induction " and nothing more—that is, an apology for their opera, so as to disarm criticism by the suggestion that what was apparently serious was really meant to be comic, or *vice versa*. Hoffmannsthal is well read in English literature, and is no doubt as familiar with *The Knight of the Burning Pestle* as he is with *The Taming of the Shrew ;* it is quite possible, too, that he is acquainted with the old Italian *Don Giovanni* opera which Mozart's clever librettist adapted to his own uses. Having borrowed poor M. Jourdain to serve the purpose of a Christopher Sly, the author and composer soon saw that it could be easy and effective from the ordinary manager's point of view to keep the most broadly comic scenes, and introduce a liberal dose of incidental music ; moreover, M. Jourdain having held the stage both in France and in Germany for a couple of centuries, those of the audience who might be bored with the opera could at least be sure of having a good deal of fun for their money out of a tabloid arrangement of Molière.

The plain fact remains, however, that in this entertainment Molière does not count artistically at all. M. Jourdain has no more appropriateness to Strauss' opera, even as a Christopher Sly, than he would have to *Fanny's First Play ;* if an induction is wanted at all, it must be an induction of our own times. The dressing up of prologue and opera in seventeenth century costume and language is merely an ingenious way of escape from the difficulties which would ensue if the problem presented was taken seriously.

Hoffmannsthal, like a great many literary and artistic people at the present day, has fallen in love with the baroque. We are all rather sick of Ruskin and St. Pancras station ; we are all beginning to think it rather amusing to play with ideas which our elders considered to be in bad taste. And it so happens that Hoffmannsthal by way of being original, has just discovered that the English theatre of the seventeenth century produced at least one immortal masterpiece—Otway's *Venice Preserved*. Here let me say that Hoffmannsthal, as a clever German, has a real and serious advantage over us English people ; he probably does not see much difference between the fine poetry and the mere bombast that are both to be found in the serious scenes, and although he can hardly appreciate the innermost flavour of the comic scenes, he at any rate has probably no scruple whatever (his version of the play is known to me only at second hand) in translating them literally, whereas in England the fantastic humours of Nacky and her Antonio have been banished from the stage since the days of George II.

As a matter of fact the jumble of high tragedy and low comedy for which Hoffmannsthal so highly commends Otway was to be found in practically every Italian opera libretto of Otway's period. Moreover, the comic episodes of the Italian operas were certainly influenced to some extent by the Comedy of Masks—the extemporised comedies of Harlequin and Pantaloon, which were acted at every village fair. *Ariadne* then, it might be inferred, is really a parody of seventeenth-century Italian opera. Well, it is just such a parody as might be written by a man who had read some casual dictionary article about Italian opera and the Comedy of Masks, but had never given a moment's study to the very copious documents that remain, or even to the very copious literature about them. It is just possible that a clever composer with an antiquarian turn of mind and a keen sense of real scholarship, such as is extremely rare in Germany, might have set Hoffmannsthal's *Ariadne* to a fairly amusing parody of old Italian music : but I cannot see that it would have been worth the trouble, given the fact that a modern audience knows nothing of the style parodical. And even if it had been worth while, there surely was never a composer less fitted for the task than Richard Strauss.

Now the sense of fine scholarship is by no means the first test of a really great composer. Or rather, a great composer may possess it, but does not make a parade of it, because the essential greatness of his thought and the clearness of his expression form a style of their own. On the other hand, the moment a composer wishes either to imitate or to parody some other composer's style, the sense of scholarship becomes indispensable. It is a quality which few composers of operas can afford to do without, since it is only the very greatest who can sustain the interest of an opera without recourse to local colour, or some analogous device. Strauss is not one of these. In spite of all his cleverness, in spite of moments of real greatness, there is hardly a work of his which does not break down somewhere from want of scholarship. As long as Strauss is writing his own serious and strenuous style, his cacophony and even his coarseness of thought can be forgiven him. It is in his moments of would-be simplicity and popularity that he is utterly intolerable. The most horrible instance of all, perhaps, occurs in *Salome*, where by way of contrast to the perversities of Herod and his court the first followers of Jesus are represented musically by phrases which recall Franz Abt and the rest of the male-voice part-song school. *Der Rosenkavalier* is so full of these vulgarities that there is no room for anything to set a higher standard to the listener. *Ariadne* is as strange a mixture as Strauss has ever produced. The incidental music to the induction might pass if Molière's play were given complete on its own merits ; it is generally agreeable and occasionally amusing in a heavy-handed sort of way. It is not particularly characteristic of Strauss, and it never for a single moment bears the least resemblance to seventeenth century music. As a musical induction to *Ariadne* it is mere waste of time.

Had Sir Herbert Tree given us the entertainment all in one language we might have had the whole of the scene which immediately precedes the opera, a scene which makes the opera a little more intelligible. It is not sufficient merely to see the horror of the composer when the order is given for the opera and the harlequinade to take place simultaneously. The offended dignity of the *prima donna* and the pert familiarity of Zerbinetta before the opera begins, go some way towards explaining their behaviours on the stage, for we are apparently meant to realise that the " opera " is merely an opera, and that the persons taking part in it are really live actors and actresses.

It is this want of sincerity, combined with the want of scholarship that constitutes the great blemish of the work. It is the more painfully noticeable, because the concluding scene of the arrival of Bacchus and his duet with Ariadne are apparently quite sincere and undoubtedly beautiful. It is here if anywhere that Strauss has developed something of a new style, and a style that is free both of commonplace and of obscurity. In the earlier part of the serious opera, where Ariadne is surrounded by the Naiad, the Dryad, and Echo, there are some beautiful effects, but they are studies in the technique of vocal writing rather than the inevitable expression of genuine emotion, either literary or musical. As for Zerbinetta and her crew, they are tedious in the extreme. The composer who could write a symphonic movement on *Funiculì funiculà* in the belief that it was a genuine folksong could hardly be expected to differentiate musically the individualities of Arlecchino, Brighella and the rest. The ensembles of male voices suggest nothing but a German *Liedertafel*. The mere difficulty of Zerbinetta's great aria has made a sensation among those who live on " sensations," but what does it amount to ? It is preceded by a recitative of real power and individuality ; a slow aria follows which oscillates between sentimental melody of Strauss' usual type when aiming at simplicity, and commonplace scales or cadenzas. After this comes the great rondo, intended apparently as a parody of Bellini, since the first phrase has a faint resemblance to *Ah mon giunge*. But Bellini, when he set out to write a tune could at any rate keep it going ; Strauss sheers off into a different style after two bars. The exaggerated *coloratura* which forms the greater part of the rondo is rarely expressive and seldom even effective. When it is not made up of obviously instrumental phrases, it is a mere string of threadbare tags from Meyerbeer. Of the real dramatic value of *coloratura* either in comedy or tragedy Strauss appears to know nothing whatever. And he is reputed to be a great Mozart scholar !

Yet we need not be without hope. One cannot hear *Ariadne in Naxos* without perceiving that Strauss is at last beginning to realise, however dimly, the expressive powers of the voice. It is a new medium to him, as it must be to any modern German composer, and he will take some time before he can express himself fully in it. He is half ashamed of it at present, and afraid that the critic will laugh at him ; that is why he hopes to get the laugh of them by throwing all the blame on the shoulders of poor M. Jourdain. It is not, however, in Zerbinetta's aria that the conversion is apparent, not in the variations on the Rhine-maidens' songs, nor in the hymn-tune trio sung towards the end by the three nymphs, but in the scene of Bacchus and Ariadne that Strauss has at last allowed his voices to be the means by which he expresses his real musical thought. It is this duet that may perhaps make *Ariadne* a work of real importance in the history of modern German music.

EPILOGUE III. BAINS TURCS By KATHERINE MANSFIELD

"THIRD storey—to the left, Madame," said the cashier, handing me a pink ticket. " One moment—I will ring for the elevator." Her black satin skirt swished across the scarlet and gold hall, and she stood among the artificial palms, her white neck and powdered face topped with masses of gleaming orange hair—like an over-ripe fungus bursting from a thick, black stem. She rang and rang. " A thousand pardons, Madame. It is disgraceful. A new attendant. He leaves this week." With her fingers on the bell she peered into the cage as though she expected to see him, lying on the floor, like a dead bird. " It is disgraceful ! " There appeared from nowhere a tiny figure disguised in a peaked cap and dirty white cotton gloves. " Here you are ! " she scolded. " Where have you been ? What have you been doing ? " For answer the figure hid its face behind one of the white cotton gloves and sneezed twice. " Ugh ! Disgusting ! Take Madame to the third storey ! " The midget stepped aside, bowed, entered after me and clashed the gates to. We ascended, very slowly, to an accompaniment of sneezes and prolonged, half whistling sniffs. I asked the top of the patent leather cap : " Have you a cold ? " " It is the air, Madame," replied the creature, speaking through its nose with a restrained air of great relish, " one is never dry here. Third floor—*if* you please," sneezing over my ten-centime tip.

I walked along a tiled corridor decorated with advertisements for lingerie and bust improvers—was allotted a tiny cabin and a blue print chemise and told to undress and find the Warm Room as soon as possible. Through the matchboard walls and from the corridor sounded cries and laughter and snatches of conversation. " Are you ready ? " " Are you coming out now ? " " Wait till you see me ! " " Berthe—Berthe ! " " One moment ! One moment! Immediately ! " I undressed quickly and carelessly, feeling like one of a troupe of little schoolgirls let loose in a swimming bath.

The Warm Room was not large. It had terra cotta painted walls with a fringe of peacocks, and a glass roof, through which one could see the sky, pale and unreal as a photographer's background screen. Some round tables strewn with shabby fashion journals, a marble basin in the centre of the room, filled with yellow lilies, and on the long, towel enveloped chairs, a number of ladies, apparently languid as the flowers. . . . I lay back with a cloth over my head, and the air, smelling of jungles and circuses and damp washing made me begin to dream. . . Yes, it might have been very fascinating to have married an explorer . . . and lived in a jungle, as long as he didn't shoot anything or take anything captive. I detest performing beasts. Oh . . . those circuses at home . . . the tent in the paddock and the children swarming over the fence to stare at the waggons and at the clown making up with his glass stuck on the waggon wheel—and the steam organ playing the *Honeysuckle and the Bee* much too fast . . . over and over. . . . I know what this air reminds me of—a game of follow my leader among the clothes hung out to dry. . . .

The door opened. Two tall blonde women in red and white check gowns came in and took the chairs opposite mine. One of them carried a box of mandarins wrapped in silver paper and the other a manicure set. They were very stout, with gay, bold faces, and quantities of exquisite whipped fair hair.

Before sitting down they glanced round the room, looked the other women up and down, turned to each other, grimaced, whispered something, and one of them said, offering the box, " Have a mandarin ? " At that they started laughing—they lay back and shook, and each time they caught sight of each other broke out afresh. " Ah, that was too good," cried one, wiping her eyes very carefully, just at the corners. " You and I, coming in here, quite serious, you know, very correct—and looking round the room—and—and as a result of our *careful* inspection—I offer you a mandarin. No, it's too funny. I must remember that. It's good enough for a music hall. Have a mandarin ? " " But I cannot imagine," said the other, " why women look so hideous in Turkish baths—like beef steaks in chemises. Is it the women—or is it the air ?

Look at that one, for instance—the skinny one, reading a book and sweating at the moustache—and those two over in the corner, discussing whether or not they ought to tell their non-existent babies how babies come—and . . . Heavens ! Look at this one coming in. Take the box, dear. Have all the mandarins."

The newcomer was a short stout little woman with flat, white feet and a black mackintosh cap over her hair. She walked up and down the room, swinging her arms, in affected unconcern, glanced contemptuously at the laughing women and rang the bell for the attendant. It was answered immediately by " Berthe," half naked and sprinkled with soapsuds. " Well, what is it, Madame. I've no time . . ." " Please bring me a hand towel," said the Mackintosh Cap, in German. " Pardon ? I do not understand. Do you speak French ? " " Non," said the mackintosh cap. " Ber—the ! " shrieked one of the blonde women, " have a mandarin. Oh, mon Dieu, I shall die of laughing." The Mackintosh Cap went through a pantomime of finding herself wet and rubbing herself dry. " *Verstehen Sie*." " Mais non, Madame," said Berthe, watching with round eyes that snapped with laughter, and she left the Mackintosh Cap, winked at the blonde women, came over, felt them as though they had been a pair of prize poultry, said " You are doing very well," and disappeared again. The Mackintosh Cap sat down on the edge of a chair, snatched a fashion journal, smacked over the crackling pages and pretended to read and the blonde women leaned back eating the mandarins and throwing the peelings into the lily basin. A scent of fruit, fresh and penetrating, hung on the air. I looked round at the other women. Yes, they were hideous, lying back, red and moist, with dull eyes and lank hair, the only little energy they had vented in shocked prudery at the behaviour of the two blondes. Suddenly I discovered Mackintosh Cap staring at me over the top of her fashion journal, so intently that I took flight and went into the hot room. But in vain ! Mackintosh Cap followed after and planted herself in front of me.

" I know," she said, confident and confiding, " that you can speak German. I saw it in your face just now. Wasn't that a scandal about the attendant refusing me a towel? I shall speak to the management about that and I shall get my husband to write them a letter this evening. Things always come better from a man, don't they? No," she said, rubbing her yellowish arms, " I've never been in such a scandalous place—and four francs fifty to pay! Naturally, I shall not give a tip. You wouldn't, would you? Not after that scandal about a hand towel. . . . I've a great mind to complain about those women as well. Those two that keep on laughing and eating. Do you know who they are?" She shook her head. " They're not respectable women—you can tell at a glance. At least I can, any married woman can. They're nothing but a couple of street women. I've never been so insulted in my life. Laughing at me, mind you! The great big fat pigs like that! And I haven't sweated at all properly, just because of them. I got so angry that the sweat turned in instead of out; it does in excitement, you know, sometimes, and now instead of losing my cold, I wouldn't be surprised if I brought on a fever."

I walked round the hot room in misery pursued by the Mackintosh Cap until the two blonde women came in, and seeing her, burst into another fit of laughter. To my rage and disgust Mackintosh Cap sidled up to me, smiled meaningly, and drew down her mouth. " I don't care," she said, in her hideous German voice. " I shouldn't lower myself by paying any attention to a couple of street women. If my husband knew he'd never get over it. Dreadfully particular he is. We've been married six years. We come from Salzburg. It's a nice town. Four children I have living, and it was really to get over the shock of the fifth that we came here. The fifth," she whispered, padding after me, " was born, a fine healthy child, and it never breathed! Well, after nine months, a woman can't help being disappointed, can she?"

I moved towards the vapour room. " Are you going in there," she said. " I wouldn't if I were you. Those two have gone in. They may think you want to strike up an acquaintance with them.

You never know, women like that." At that moment they came out, wrapping themselves in the rough gowns, and passing Mackintosh Cap like disdainful queens. " Are you going to take your chemise off in the vapour room ? " asked she. " Don't mind me, you know. Woman is woman, and besides, if you'd rather, I won't look at you. I know—I used to be like that. I wouldn't mind betting," she went on savagely, " those filthy women had a good look at each other. Pooh ! women like that. You can't shock them. And don't they look dreadful. Bold and all that false hair. That manicure box one of them had was fitted up with gold. Well, I don't suppose it was real, but I think it was disgusting to bring it. One might at least cut one's nails in private, don't you think ? I *cannot* see," she said, " what men see in such women. No, a husband and children and a home to look after, that's what a woman needs. That's what my husband says. Fancy one of these hussies peeling potatoes or choosing the meat ! Are you going already ? "

I flew to find Berthe and all the time I was soaped and smacked and sprayed and thrown in a cold water tank I could not get out of my mind the ugly, wretched figure of the little German with a good husband and four children railing against the two fresh beauties who had never peeled potatoes nor chosen the right meat. In the anteroom I saw them once again. They were dressed in blue. One was pinning on a bunch of violets, the other buttoning a pair of ivory suede gloves. In their charming feathered hats and furs they stood talking. " Yes, there they are," said a voice at my elbow. And Mackintosh Cap, transformed, in a blue and white check blouse and crochet collar, with the little waist and large hips of the German woman and a terrible bird nest, which Salzburg doubtless called *Reise Hut* on her head. " How do you suppose they can afford clothes like that ? The horrible, low creatures. No, they're enough to make a young girl think twice." And as the two walked out of the anteroom, Mackintosh Cap stared after them, her sallow face all mouth and eyes, like the face of a hungry child before a forbidden table.

CHRONICLES OF THE MONTH

THE THEATRE

By GILBERT CANNAN

Masefield and Marie Lloyd.

IT is tolerably certain that Marie Lloyd has never read a word of Masefield, nor could her art gain anything from the study of his. Mr. Masefield, on the other hand, could gain considerably in the technique of the theatre by a critical examination of the greatest of comedienne's rendering, as Mother Eve, of the couplets :

> " When once I ate an apple the whole universe was stirred,
> Now girls can eat bananas and no one says a word."

The suggestion is not, of course, that such words should be put into the mouth of Nan or that Nan should be turned into a figure in any way resembling Marie Lloyd, though, for the purposes of burlesque, that would be an excellent expedient. The reason for this apparently grotesque juxtaposition of names is that I left the performance of *Nan* with a certain amount of dissatisfaction and found, or thought I found, the explanation of it when I listened to Marie Lloyd a few nights later. Years ago, when I attended the first performance of *Nan* at the Royalty Theatre—the play having been rejected even by the Stage Society, God bless it—I had this same feeling of dissatisfaction, though perhaps in a greater degree, and I suffered from it more because I was unpractised in the analysis of stage effects and miscalculations. I felt the beauty of the play, its curious athletic leaps into beauty, but I also felt that this beauty was withheld from me, not artfully, so as to lead me on to higher and purer realms, but inadvertently. Then the play was not particularly well acted, and its dramatic quality was ruthlessly sacrificed to the Gaffer, whose description of the tide boring up the Severn was treated as the highest point of the tragedy, rather like building a house for the sake of an ornament over the drawing-room window. At the Court Theatre, the other day, the play was in much better focus and the part of Nan was superbly played by Miss Irene Rooke, with a beauty of tone and gesture and a skill in skating over the sentimental passages that I cannot remember to have seen equalled. The rendering of the noblest scene in the play, the love-passage between Nan and Dick Gurvil is surely the finest, almost the only real achievement in the modern English theatre (leaving Ireland out of account), and the names of Mr. Milton Rosmer and Miss Irene Rooke should mark a stage in the revival of English acting, as that of Mr. Masefield marks a stage in the renaissance of poetry and the drama. I would like to leave it at that, but I must work back to Marie Lloyd and my thesis, which has grown out of the feeling of disgust that followed on the moment of delight occasioned by that scene and its rendering. The love scene in *Nan* is followed by one of the worst scenes in modern drama, that between Dick and Mrs. Pargetter. It is incompetent and throws the audience back into listlessness and bewilderment. It comes, I fancy, from distrust of the emotional and imaginative force of the play and inability to shake off the old superstition that a play's technical machinery is something entirely separate from its contents. That is only true when a play has no contents and is born of no imaginative necessity. *Nan* is a strange play in that it is streaked with imagination rather than informed with it. It seems definitely to belong to a transitional period and to be half art, half old conventions. However, if it is not completely beautiful in itself, it is the occasion of much beautiful and really moving acting. Actors, of course, ask no more of dramatists than that. Audiences ask a great deal more, and they get it in the music-halls at the hands of the best and, be it noted, the most successful performers. Marie Lloyd's work for instance, is simply astonishing in its finish and subtlety and ease. Her material is often very poor, but she never utters a word nor makes a gesture that does not contribute in the minds of her audience to the general impression of wit. It is not enough for her, she knows, simply to be Marie Lloyd, but she must be from moment to moment Marie Lloyd in the terms of her audience's general anticipation of pleasure. A reputation helps, of course. Jack Point has only to say " Pass the mustard " to be greeted with roars of laughter, but he has to say it in Jack Point's way, with no technical fumbling. A first-rate artist will recognise that his reputation is other people's affair and not his own, and will not regard it as a part of his equipment. A second-rate artist will and nearly always does regard his reputation as a fetish, and devotes all his energies to feeding it, sacrificing everything, even his art, even his audience to it. Marie Lloyd is a first-rate artist. She has real wit and spontaneity and is therefore a touchstone for other works of art, even in a different kind, even for tragedy and poetry. I commend her work to the study of Mr. Masefield. It does throw light on dramatic work of all kinds, even on the works of William Shakespeare, who would have loved her and added her to his splendid collection of funny females. She would have called him " Bill " and he would have liked it. I should love to see her call Mr. Masefield " Jack," and to see him enjoy it.

Security and Adventure.

I

MR. WINSTON CHURCHILL in his novel " The Inside of the Cup " has given his many readers precisely what his many readers desire.

Mr. Churchill has, for a number of years, now been heavily lumbering along in his slow-moving, solid and practical conveyance and we have greeted his very solidity as a relief. He has given us, once in every two years, a hard chunk of American social history, introducing us to men and women whose boots and overcoats are admirably convincing; with heavy, solemn tread, no smile upon his face, his gaze a little anxious, his chin confidently raised, Mr. Churchill has solemnly displayed his histories. . . .

I had shared for a number of years in that comfortable arm-chair reality that had pleased so many of my acquaintances. There was, for one thing, no danger, no startling imagination, no ironic phrase, no beauty suddenly revealed could jump the nerves—only, always, I knew that that sedate and companionable voice would murmur on for my slothful entertainment.

Now, suddenly, with " The Inside of the Cup " the desire for that security has vanished. I am bored, indifferent, impatient. Perhaps in this account of American religious disturbances, Mr. Churchill is heavier, more solid, than ever before; perhaps the need for another " Robert Elsmere " has passed; perhaps sentences like " Hodder's eyes were arrested by a crowd, barring the sidewalk on the block ahead " or vivid description like " Behind the house, in the sunlight, were massed spruces of a brilliant arsenic green with purple cones " had an unsympathetic effect; perhaps the frontispiece that shows us Mr. Hodder's anguish as he is asked by a lady friend, " Can't you *feel* that you are an individual, a personality, a force that might be put to great uses," told me that Mr. Hodder's history would be unsatisfactory.

It is enough that Mr. Churchill has allowed his interest in

questions of modern theology to overwhelm both his sense of humour and his knowledge of human nature. His book is dull, lifeless, void.

Nevertheless there is this interesting fact about it that its solid security is precisely what a very great number of people desire. Mr. Churchill is, in his books, so safe, so sure, so certainly to be relied upon that there can never be any kind of question as to his success. If he wants to tell us about a sidewalk or an arsenic green house he tells us without a tremor, without exaggeration, or extravagance. If he wants to tell us about the troubles in a clergyman's soul or the unhappiness of a lady of pleasure he tells us quite simply with words exactly suited to his vision. This placid perfection, this assured definition is as near to art as the Eiffel Tower is to Chartres Cathedral, but it is always visible, always tangible, always assured of its importance. What would happen to Mr. Churchill did he have a sudden revelation, were he to behold pigs flying or the statue of Liberty floating happily down New York harbour it is terrible to consider.

Meanwhile he is magnificently safe . . .

II

With what an anxious eye would he gaze upon Miss Sheila Kaye-Smith or Mr. D. H. Lawrence, were he informed of their perilous existences. Such works as "Isle of Thorns" or "Sons and Lovers" must seem to him the maddest and most irresponsible adventures. He would, in fact, be quite justified in considering that the Raphael of Miss Kaye-Smith or the Paul Morel of Mr. Lawrence were dim and uncertain figures beside his own Mr. Hodder. Mr. Hodder's clerical hat is as certain as the days of the week; Raphael and Paul are dimly and most strangely clothed . . .

The dividing-line is here. Mr. Churchill has his public, his message, his sure reward. Miss Kaye-Smith and Mr. Lawrence have, in comparison, a small public, no message, and a reward that is their own private affair. Meanwhile they are engaged upon most thrilling adventures.

" Isle of Thorns " is the fourth of Miss Kaye-Smith's novels and is worthy to stand with its predecessors. Perhaps " Starbrace " is still the most satisfying of these volumes, and I am not sure that " The Tramping Methodist " did not, five years ago, carry one as far along the road as " Isle of Thorns " does now, but to anyone who does not know the earlier novels " Isle of Thorns " must come as a fine shining experience, a work that, with some faults and a number of uncertainties, arrives very nearly as a great romance of the first class.

It is, I believe, the very uncertainty of Miss Kaye-Smith's touch that is the most hopeful element in her work. Amongst the younger novelists she stands alone for the inspiration of her vision. That inspiration sometimes fails her, but she is less dependant than any of her contemporaries, on her own past experiences. She creates simply by the fine energy of her imagination ; at times, as now in the character of Sally, that imagination refuses conviction. Sally is real at moments only, and her relations with Baird and Raphael are clouded by the failure of her own spontaneous movements. In evolving her, Miss Kaye-Smith has been forced to work her imagination instead of allowing that imagination to do as it will. Sally is only half imagined. But Raphael—his tramp, his son, his charming priggishness—is a triumph of character : Miss Kaye-Smith has found him without being told that she ought to find him. The adventure came to her.

The Fair, the Sussex country, the hedges and skies and fields, lights and darkness, these things colour, without false sentiment or purple effects, her pages. She is, in all things, a true artist.

III

Mr. Lawrence is also an artist and " Sons and Lovers," in the first part of it at any rate, demands our most serious admiration. The pages that have to do with the early Morel history, with Mrs.

Morel, Mr. Morel (a magnificent sketch), young Paul, William and the others, are finer than anything that the younger novelists have given us since James Douglas' " House with the Green Shutters."

I am reminded of that earlier work by Mr. Lawrence's combination of hard realism and passionate colour. There is much here that bites hard into the page and seems to stain it deep with its fine pungent reality. Little things Mr. Lawrence can array in fine procession. " The meadows seemed one space of ripe, evening light, whispering with the distant mill-race. She sat on a seat under the alders in the cricket ground, and fronted the evening. Before her, level and solid, spread the big green cricket-field, like the bed of a sea of light. Children played in the bluish shadow of the pavilion. Many rooks, high up, came cawing home across the softly woven sky. They stooped in a long curve down into the golden glow, concentrating, cawing, wheeling, like black flakes on a slow vortex, over a tree-clump that made a dark boss among the pasture."

I have quoted that at length because this passionate beauty is on every page and close against it passionate ugliness, grit, grime, vice, disorder, unhappiness . . . Behind it all there is this zest. This is the new thing that Mr. Lawrence is bringing to the English novel, a flaming excitement about everything in the world. " Leaves of Grass " rise to one's mind as this fine catalogue is proclaimed; it seems to me now that Walt Whitman's poetry is the only proper parallel to Mr. Lawrence's " Sons and Lovers."

But it is precisely because I feel that parallel that I am not sure whether Mr. Lawrence is yet a novelist. The supreme duty and purpose of the novelist as distinguished from the poet and the essayist is the creation of character, and it is here that Mr. Lawrence fails.

Very fine is the inception of Mrs. Morel, but as the book progresses and Paul is caught into his amorous adventures, Mrs. Morel slips away. Surely it had been Mr. Lawrence's purpose to discover his book's motive in the struggle between the mother and the lover for Paul. That struggle, eagerly anticipated by the reader, is lost in Mr. Lawrence's discoveries. Here is a scene, here an experience, here a colour or a scent . . . always these things, the thrilling jumble and collision of life, catch Mr. Lawrence's attention. Paul, himself, is never bound finally together. We are shown him here and there, are told of his impulses, his desires, but the ultimate picture that we should have of him is never given to us.

Finally there are in this book too many physical experiences. It is not that such things are of small importance, but it is rather that the repetition of them overbalances the book's proportions. It is this excess that is Mr. Lawrence's chief danger.

Here, however, in " Isle of Thorns " and " Sons and Lovers " are two books, courageous, honest, adventurous. Introduce Mr. Hodder and his theology to Raphael and Paul Morel and how good for him these new friends would be !

GENERAL LITERATURE By FRANK SWINNERTON

Irish Plays and Playwrights: Lady Gregory's New Comedies: The Joy of the Theatre

MR. PETT RIDGE, in a passage almost excusably underlined and over-quoted, made a stout lady exclaim, after hearing "Kathleen Mavourneen" sung: "Anything about Ireland always makes me cry: I come from Kent." That remark, over-emphasised though it is into travesty, does nevertheless show that Mr. Pett Ridge's sense of things is not so purely grotesque and derivative as some readers are in the habit of suggesting. It shows that he is not unaware of piercing general truths; one of which is that there is prevalent in England a shocking sentimentality over the subject of Ireland. Mournful Irish songs produce free tears, however bad the songs may be. Songs such as "Come Back to Erin" are as popular with the general public as "Father O'Flynn." At the time of the Boer War one of the songs that moved drunken men most easily to tears was "What do you think of the Irish now?"

From the easily moved drunkard to the enthusiast in other fields is not a very great step. In the theatre the case is only on a different level. Of course, lovers of sentimental songs find themselves driven away by the Irish drama (excepting by the farces of Lady Gregory, which are sufficiently clear to be acceptable by all minds); but there is nevertheless a danger that in our love of the beautiful tones and phrases we may be misled into thinking that whatever comes out of Ireland must be first rate. The cause of English loyalty to Ireland is the fact that the English, having lost nationality in empire, look with wonder at a nation within that empire—no longer puzzled and sullen, but proud of every part of its heritage. Where the history of England in the nineteenth century embraces a bewildering host of petty bullyings and stupidities and clumsy sad dismays and errors, the history of Ireland (read either with or without *parti pris*) is a record of splendid lost endeavour. Nothing so quickly touches the heart and moves swift enthusiasm as lost endeavour.

It is without avail that Mr. Shaw "exposes" the Irish, or that some of the later Irish dramatists painstakingly dwell in the shady walks of the national life. The enthusiasm has kindled : the English are on the whole more prone to excite themselves about the Irish—as a character, or as a nation, or as an art-producing colony—than they are about any other (even the most distant) section of the empire. It was to be, and is ; and all we can do now is to try to discriminate between the real virtues of the Irish and those virtues which have been plastered on to the Irish by our own solemn superficiality.

In America the transplanted Irish grew angry with the greatest modern play ; but there has sprung up there as here a parasitic literature, founded upon the writings of Ireland. I do not refer to such books as Mr. P. P. Howe's study of Synge, which is profoundly critical as well as enthusiastic. But I may perhaps allow myself to describe Mr. Cornelius Weygandt's book ("Irish Plays and Playwrights," Constable, 6*s*. 6*d*. net) as a curious mixture of shrewd criticism and preposterous comment, due in part to a ravenous desire for completeness and in part to an inability to find the exact criticism for each item under survey. Mr. Weygandt is obsessed by what he insists upon calling "The Celtic Renaissance," and the index to his book shows a perfectly amazing industry in the reading and correlation of poets, playwrights, and novelists. But although a sixth of the whole work is taken up with a huge estimate of the works of William Sharp, and although Ibsen and Maeterlinck are freely referred to, one may go the whole length of the book and fail to find mention of the fact that Goldsmith and Mangan were Irishmen, while such modern writers as James Stephens, Winifred Letts, and Lord Dunsany are either practically or wholly ignored. I should not personally have included Goldsmith as a participant in the Celtic Renaissance ; but Mr. Weygandt is at pains to show that George Moore is the only great

Irish novelist because Miss Edgeworth is not the equal of Miss Austen. Apart from the fact that the sex of a writer is not the only thing to be considered in comparative criticism, it may also be said that Miss Edgeworth was a very good novelist indeed, and that in any case the introduction of her name (and the names of many other persons of like irrelevance) has not a great deal to do with the Irish literary movement. The truth is that Mr. Weygandt has not kept to the title of his book because he wanted to rope in all he knew about Irish literature. That has been his undoing. Instead of taking the spirit of each writer and illustrating his criticism by examples chosen for the purpose, he seems to take every work in turn and to attempt some apt criticism upon it. The supply of *aperçus* proves on the whole to be very unequal to the demand, and Mr. Weygandt goes bothering round a point until he is really smothered by his own unhappy method. Thus, in the essay on Synge, we get this comical hotch-potch, which goes gravely from one irrelevant comparison to another—" Borrow, who comes to mind more often than any other writer as one reads Synge, chose to avoid love scenes, and Borrow's follower, Mr. Hewlett, for all his gusto, has no such exaltation as this. Had Harry Richmond taken to the road with Kiomi we might have known something like it. A chapter out of the early life of Juggling Jerry and his ' Old Girl,' done in the manner of ' Love in the Valley,' would be still nearer to it. . . . I doubt if Synge had read Meredith, and even had he, the life of the roads and their cottages that Synge knew so well was his master, and no writer at all." So that all these suppositions bring us to an admission of their futility. Mr. Weygandt is not often as bad as this ; but his book would have been better if it had aimed at being simply a critical study of its subject, and not a meandering stream of often perfunctory commentary.

I said that Lady Gregory had the power to please English sentimentalists who were affronted by Synge. By this I did not mean that Lady Gregory was sentimental. Her work has a quite admirable freedom from sentimentality, and her notes to a new volume (" New Plays," Putnam, 5*s.* net) are full of sage remarks. The plays themselves are similar to those which we have previously seen, and perhaps the best of them is " Damer's Gold," a two-act comedy. One, " Coats," is in Lady Gregory's less happy style, an antic squabble which resembles in its chattering style such a play as " The Workhouse Ward." These plays produce much laughter in the theatre ; but they are not really amusing. Lady Gregory says that she began to write comedies because they were needed for the Abbey Theatre ; and even such plays as " Hyacinth Halvey " and (in the new volume) " The Full Moon " have a thin body of funning rather than a genuine humorous impulse. For the reason that it is based upon a moral idea, and that verbal eccentricity is less sought after in the speeches, I think " Damer's Field " is the best play in the new volume. It has some character, and is strictly worked out. That cannot be said of " The Bogie Man," with its flail-like speeches ; although the idea is genuinely comic. But Lady Gregory is really a serious dramatist, and not a writer of farcical dialogues ; and it is when she is furthest away from caricature that her work is most characteristic.

Mr. Gilbert Cannan has contributed to Mr. Batsford's charming new series of " Fellowship Books " (2*s.* net per volume) a very refreshing essay on " The Joy of the Theatre." Mr. Cannan is intensely hopeful, looking to the future for the realisation of his dreams ; and it is delightful to find him so generous in acknowledging good work, however far it may be in its aims from his own ideal. Mr. Cannan's book is practically an appeal on behalf of the artist. He wants the artist to take joy in the making of beautiful things for their own sake. Only so can art be truly a creative force. This, naturally, is difficult at the present time, when we are but slightly emergent from a reaction against insincerity ; but Mr. Cannan has a clear perception of encouraging signs. When he so obviously looks to the younger generation for further advances along the splendid road to a new artistic era, the younger generation cannot but accept the challenge—not because it is Mr. Cannan who demands support, but because Mr. Cannan's is the immediate voice that speaks. But it is impossible to avoid finding some peculiar fascination in ugliness for its own sake : if it is the sense of beauty that makes the artist self-expressive, it is the sense of ugliness that tempers his rapture, and gives it the quality of fine steel. Synge is full of the sense of ugliness no less than the sense of beauty ; and if these things are in his work lightened by the most wonderful power of imagining and transmitting the fine quality of joy, we must not omit to record their presence. Some of the other Irish dramatists have no joy ; they are guilty of tame acquiescence in a movement, a serious dependance upon the acting of the Abbey company for an effect of reality. This is not as it should be. They have actors whose powers seem equal to all demands ; they have a loyal audience of their countrymen abroad, and the beastly patronage of the polite class, plus the sentiment of the Celtomaniac. Yet even Mr. Weygandt, although he seems to have hunted through the work of the minor Irish dramatists with characteristic vigilance and mildly-exerted enthusiasm, is forced to hesitate. It is one of the worst points of his book that he goes through everything and leaves the reader without any conclusions ; but it does appear more or less distinctly that only one or two of the young men are doing work to warrant inclusion in a " Celtic Renaissance." On the evidence, the Renaissance has outgrown its strength, by being over-cultivated. What Mr. Cannan wants, and what we all want, is an art that bites through the surface of life as a beginning—something with vitality, no matter how that vitality may be directed. In the modern Irish drama there is little vitality, and it is still so much the fashion to cry at anything Irish (or to laugh) that it will be some time before we realise that what edifies us in the performances of modern Irish plays is the presentation, not the fine heart of joy which we think is there. Synge had the joy Mr. Cannan wants, and his splendid preface to " The Tinker's Wedding " is quoted appropriately in Mr. Cannan's book. But where else in all this boasted Celtic Renaissance has joy any place ? Mr. Yeats is a great poet ; Mr. James Stephens has a daring and amazing personality ; but beyond these names the Irish literary movement is often enough a sad and spiritless affair. We have got in England (though we make no boast of it, and have no books written about it) a dramatic movement of equal strength. We have men who are really striking out new paths, and trying to go beyond their sincere predecessors both in sincerity and in creative power. Only the appalling sentimentality and false judgment which the Irish habitually arouse in England is responsible for the great over-praising of the Irish literary movement. We shall have many more fat books about the Celtic Renaissance ; and apart from Synge as a dramatist and Mr. Yeats as a poet there will always be the need to fill the book with essays on William Sharp or some other persons who have nothing to do with the case. The sooner Mr. Cannan's joy is triumphantly found in the English theatre, the sooner we shall—dramatically speaking—get going ; and then perhaps the rise to eminence of the English school will provoke the Irish dramatists who are writing dull plays about morbidly uninteresting people into some sort of counter-Renaissance. Otherwise, we shall continue to be sentimental about the Irish (who are sometimes, but not often, sentimental about themselves) until the conceited nation will assume that the names plastered on to a loyal and enthusiastic little body of workers have been really earned. The Celtic Renaissance is really a false term, and it does harm by exalting into a titanic struggle what is really a movement among very modern, very thoughtful, and very derivative amateurs.

GERMAN BOOKS By D. H. LAWRENCE

Thomas Mann

THOMAS MANN is perhaps the most famous of German novelists now writing. He, and his elder brother, Heinrich Mann, with Jakob Wassermann, are acclaimed the three artists in fiction of present-day Germany.

But Germany is now undergoing that craving for form in fiction, that passionate desire for the mastery of the medium of narrative, that will of the writer to be greater than and undisputed lord over the stuff he writes, which is figured to the world in Gustave Flaubert.

Thomas Mann is over middle age, and has written three or four books : " Buddenbrooks," a novel of the patrician life of Lübeck ; " Tristan," a collection of six " Novellen " ; " Konigliche Hoheit," an unreal Court romance ; various stories, and lastly, " Der Tod in Venedig." The author himself is the son of a Lübeck " Patrizier."

It is as an artist rather than as a story-teller that Germany worships Thomas Mann. And yet it seems to me, this craving for form is the outcome, not of artistic conscience, but of a certain attitude to life. For form is not a personal thing like style. It is impersonal like logic. And just as the school of Alexander Pope was logical in its expressions, so it seems the school of Flaubert is, as it were, logical in its æsthetic form. " Nothing outside the definite line of the book," is a maxim. But can the human mind fix absolutely the definite line of a book, any more than it can fix absolutely any definite line of action for a living being ?

Thomas Mann, however, is personal, almost painfully so, in his subject-matter. In " Tonio Kröger," the long " Novelle " at the end of the " Tristan " volume, he paints a detailed portrait of himself as a youth and younger man, a careful analysis. And he expresses at some length the misery of being an artist. " Literature is not a calling, it is a curse." Then he says to the Russian painter girl : " There is no artist anywhere but longs again, my love, for the common life." But any young artist might say that. It is because the stress of life in a young man, but particularly in an artist, is very strong, and has as yet found no outlet, so that it rages inside him in " Sturm und Drang." But the condition is the same, only more tragic, in the Thomas Mann of fifty-three. He has never found any outlet for himself, save his art. He has never given himself to anything but his art. This is all well and good, if his art absorbs and satisfies him, as it has done some great men, like Corot. But then there are the other artists, the more human, like Shakespeare and Goethe, who must give themselves to life as well as to art. And if these were afraid, or despised life, then with their surplus they would ferment and become rotten. Which is what ails Thomas Mann. He is physically ailing, no doubt. But his complaint is deeper : it is of the soul.

And out of this soul-ailment, this unbelief, he makes his particular art, which he describes, in Tonio Kröger, as " Wählerisch, erlesen, kostbar, fein, reizbar gegen das Banale, und aufs höchste empfindlich in Fragen des Taktes und Geschmacks." He is a disciple, in method, of the Flaubert who wrote : " I worked sixteen hours yesterday, to-day the whole day, and have at last finished one page." In writing of the Leitmotiv and its influence, he says : " Now this method alone is sufficient to explain my slowness. It is the result neither of anxiety nor indigence, but of an overpowering sense of responsibility for the choice of every word, the coining of every phrase . . . a responsibility that longs for perfect freshness, and which, after two hours' work, prefers not to undertake an important sentence. For which sentence is important, and which not ? Can one know beforehand whether a sentence, or part of a sentence may not be called upon to appear again as motiv, peg, symbol, citation or connection ? And a sentence which must be heard twice must be fashioned accordingly. It must—I do not speak of beauty—possess a certain high level, and symbolic suggestion, which will make it worthy to sound again in any epic future. So every point becomes a standing ground, every adjective a decision, and it is clear that such work is not to be produced off-hand."

This, then, is the method. The man himself was always delicate in constitution. " The doctors said he was too weak to go to school, and must work at home." I quote from Aschenbach, in " Der Tod in Venedig." " When he fell, at the age of fifty-three, one of his closest observers said of him : " Aschenbach has always lived like this "—and he gripped his fist hard clenched ; " never like this " —and he let his open hand lie easily on the arm of the chair."

He forced himself to write, and kept himself to the work. Speaking of one of his works, he says : " It was pardonable, yea, it showed plainly the victory of his morality, that the uninitiated reader supposed the book to have come of a solid strength and one long breath ; whereas it was the result of small daily efforts and hundreds of single inspirations."

And he gives the sum of his experience in the belief—"dass beinahe alles Grosse, was dastehe, als ein Trotzdem dastehe, trotz Kummer und Qual, Armut, Verlassenheit, Körperschwäche, Laster, Leidenschaft und tausand hemmnischen Zustande gekommen sei." And then comes the final revelation, difficult to translate. He is speaking of life as it is written into his books :

" For endurance of one's fate, grace in suffering, does not only mean passivity, but is an active work, a positive triumph, and the Sebastian figure is the most beautiful symbol, if not of all art, yet of the art in question. If one looked into this portrayed world and saw the elegant self-control that hides from the eyes of the world to the last moment the inner undermining, the biological decay; saw the yellow ugliness which, sensuously at a disadvantage, could blow its choking heat of desire to a pure flame, and even rise to sovereignty in the kingdom of beauty ; saw the pale impotence which draws out of the glowing depths of its intellect sufficient strength to subdue a whole vigorous people, bring them to the foot of the Cross, to the feet of impotence ; saw the amiable bearing in the empty and severe service of Form ; saw the quickly enervating longing and art of the born swindler : if one saw such a fate as this, and all the rest it implied, then one would be forced to doubt whether there were in reality any other heroism than that of weakness. Which heroism, in any case, is more of our time than this ? "

Perhaps it is better to give the story of " Der Tod in Venedig," from which the above is taken, and to whose hero it applies.

Gustav von Aschenbach, a fine, famous author, over fifty years of age, coming to the end of a long walk one afternoon, sees as he is approaching a burying place, near Munich, a man standing between the chimeric figures of the gateway. This man in the gate of the cemetery is almost the motive of the story. By him, Aschenbach is infected with a desire to travel. He examines himself minutely, in a way almost painful in its frankness, and one sees the whole soul of this author of fifty-three. And it seems, the artist has absorbed the man, and yet the man is there, like an exhausted organism on which a parasite has fed itself strong. Then begins a kind of Holbein " Totentanz." The story is quite natural in appearance, and yet there is the gruesome sense of symbolism throughout. The man near the burying ground has suggested travel—but whither ? Aschenbach sets off to a watering place on the Austrian coast of the Adriatic, seeking some adventure, some passionate adventure, to which his sick soul and unhealthy body have been kindled. But finding himself on the Adriatic, he knows it is not thither that his desire draws him, and he takes ship for Venice. It is all real, and yet with a curious sinister unreality, like decay, the " biological decay." On board there is a man who reminds one of the man in the gateway, though there is no connection. And then, among a crowd of young Poles who are crossing, is a ghastly fellow, whom Aschenbach sees is an old man dressed up as young, who capers unsuspected among the youths, drinks hilariously with them, and falls hideously drunk at last on the deck, reaching to the author, and slobbering about " dem allerliebsten, dem schönsten Liebchen." Suddenly the upper plate of his false teeth falls on his underlip.

Aschenbach takes a gondola to the Lido, and again the gondolier reminds one of the man in the cemetery gateway. He is, moreover, one who will make no concession, and, in spite of Aschenbach's demand to be taken back to St. Mark's, rows him in his black craft to the Lido, talking to himself softly all the while. Then he goes without payment.

The author stays in a fashionable hotel on the Lido. The adventure is coming, there by the pallid sea. As Aschenbach comes down into the hall of the hotel, he sees a beautiful Polish boy of about fourteen, with honey-coloured curls clustering round his pale face, standing with his sisters and their governess.

Aschenbach loves the boy—but almost as a symbol. In him he loves life and youth and beauty, as Hyacinth in the Greek myth. This, I suppose, is blowing the choking heat to pure flame, and raising it to the kingdom of beauty. He follows the boy, watches him all day long on the beach, fascinated by beauty concrete before him. It is still the Künstler and his abstraction : but there is also the " yellow ugliness, sensually at a disadvantage," of the elderly man below it all. But the picture of the writer watching the folk on the beach gleams and lives with a curious, gold-phosphorescent light, touched with the brightness of Greek myth, and yet a modern sea-shore with folk on the sands, and a half-threatening, diseased sky.

Aschenbach, watching the boy in the hotel lift, finds him delicate, almost ill, and the thought that he may not live long fills the elderly writer with a sense of peace. It eases him to think the boy should die.

Then the writer suffers from the effect of the Sirocco, and intends to depart immediately from Venice. But at the station he finds with joy that his luggage has gone wrong, and he goes straight back to the hotel. There, when he sees Tadzin again, he knows why he could not leave Venice.

There is a month of hot weather, when Aschenbach follows Tadzin about, and begins to receive a look, loving, from over the lad's shoulder. It is wonderful, the heat, the unwholesomeness, the passion in Venice. One evening comes a street singer, smelling of carbolic acid, and sings beneath the verandah of the hotel. And this time, in gruesome symbolism, it is the man from the burying ground distinctly.

The rumour is, that the black cholera is in Venice. An atmos phere of secret plague hangs over the city of canals and palaces. Aschenbach verifies the report at the English bureau, but cannot bring himself to go away from Tadzin, nor yet to warn the Polish family. The secretly pest-smitten days go by. Aschenbach follows the boy through the stinking streets of the town and loses him. And on the day of the departure of the Polish family, the famous author dies of the plague.

It is absolutely, almost intentionally, unwholesome. The man is sick, body and soul. He portrays himself as he is, with wonderful skill and art portrays his sickness. And since any genuine portrait is valuable, this book has its place. It portrays one man, one atmosphere, one sick vision. It claims to do no more. And we have to allow it. But we know it is unwholesome—it does not strike me as being morbid for all that, it is too well done—and we give it its place as such.

Thomas Mann seems to me the last sick sufferer from the complaint of Flaubert. The latter stood away from life as from a leprosy. And Thomas Mann, like Flaubert, feels vaguely that he has in him something finer than ever physical life revealed. Physical life is a disordered corruption, against which he can fight with only one weapon, his fine æsthetic sense, his feeling for beauty, for perfection, for a certain fitness which soothes him, and gives him an inner pleasure, however corrupt the stuff of life may be. There he is, after all these years, full of disgusts and loathing of himself as Flaubert was, and Germany is being voiced, or partly so, by him. And so, with real suicidal intention, like Flaubert's, he sits, a last too-sick disciple, reducing himself grain by grain to the statement of his own disgust, patiently, self-destructively, so that his statement at least may be perfect in a world of corruption. But he is so late.

Already I find Thomas Mann, who, as he says, fights so hard against the banale in his work, somewhat banale. His expression may be very fine. But by now what he expresses is stale. I think we have learned our lesson, to be sufficiently aware of the fulsomeness of life. And even while he has a rhythm in style, yet his work has none of the rhythm of a living thing, the rise of a poppy, then the after uplift of the bud, the shedding of the calyx and the spreading wide of the petals, the falling of the flower and the pride of the seed-head. There is an unexpectedness in this such as does not come from their carefully plotted and arranged developments. Even " Madame Bovary " seems to me dead in respect to the living rhythm of the whole work. While it is there in "Macbeth" like life itself.

But Thomas Mann is old—and we are young. Germany does not feel very young to me.

ITALIAN BOOKS By SYDNEY WATERLOW

WHY is writing, to say nothing of painting and music, dead in modern Italy? Here is an instructive incident. In a recent number of *La Voce*, there appeared a letter from a Mr. Gustavo Botta accusing a journalist, Mr. Giuseppe Vannicola, of shameless plagiarism; Mr. Vannicola was said to have signed his name to a number of articles on such subjects as Cubism and Debussy's music which were nothing but translations and compilations clumsily made from the work of well-known French writers. The eye of M. André Gide, the novelist, critic and dramatist, who happened to be passing through Florence at the moment, was caught by this letter; dipping his pen in the acid of that refined irony which has won him so many admirers all over Europe, he wrote to the editor of *La Voce* in deprecation of Mr. Botta's outburst. What, he asked, was all this fuss about? The artistic relations between France and Italy have ever been of the most cordial; the Frenchmen from whom D'Annunzio deigns to borrow only feel themselves honoured; recently a sketch of his own was adopted by Mr. F. M. Martini for the Roman stage without acknowledgment; such incidents only foster international good-feeling. No doubt, he added, the writers pillaged by Mr. Vannicola would join, if they knew of it, in protesting indignantly against Mr. Botta's attack. The letter, in short, was a model of discreet sarcasm. What followed is almost incredible. First Mr. Botta retorts with lofty morality, explaining at immense length that it is not a question of the more or less gratification of the plagiarised, since something higher, the principle of literary honesty, is at stake, and giving in parallel columns chapter and verse for Mr. Vannicola's sins. At the same time appears a friend of the accused, a Mr. Giovanni Amendola, to thank M. Gide publicly for his spirited defence of Mr. Botta's victim. Nor does the joke end here. Mr. Botta returns to the charge with a " nothing can alter the facts "; Mr. Martini writes to say that M. Gide is no gentleman and that he himself is a gentleman—didn't he, when his play was printed, give it a motto out of one of M. Gide's works ? and finally Mr. Vannicola comes out with his defence, which is this : " There are plagiarisms of the spirit far more immoral than any plagiarisms of the letter. . . . I love life, and, in spite of painful adventures, life has not ceased to love me. My literary work has, for me, the importance of the flower which I put in my buttonhole."

Mr. Vannicola, with his bad taste in buttonholes, may be left to the obscurity which is his due ; but *La Voce* purports to be an " advanced " organ, and the controversy, however trifling, may help us to see why Italian literature is what it is to-day. The striking fact is the denseness of all the persons concerned, their entire lack of a sense of humour. Not one of them sees that M. Gide is laughing at them ; they are a pack of solemn children, egged on to absurdity by a clever, malicious grown-up. Then their fundamental insincerity, both of word and act, is obvious ; they cannot play fair, and they cannot speak except in the cadences of a hollow and insipid rhetoric. And lastly, it is only too true, " there are plagiarisms of the spirit more immoral than any plagiarism of the letter." Most Italian novels and poems of the moment are plagiarisms, not wholesome and deliberate, but subtly, as by some spiritual infusion, from French sources. The countrymen of Boccaccio, from whose wide humanity, from whose sensitiveness to the ludicrous, the beautiful and the terrible all modern narrative art is descended, seem to have lost the power of contemplating life with sincerity and independence, at least as far as the reproduction of it in words is concerned.

To begin with the question of humour, it is lack of humour which weighs down Mr. Vergilio Brocchi, author of *L'Isola Sonante* and *I Sentieri della Vita* (Milan, Fratelli Treves). Such a story, for instance, as that called *La buon' anima di Agnese*, in which a widower, bereaved in the prime of his age and burdened with a pug-dog to which the excellent defunct had been devoted, believes that life must henceforth be forlorn and impracticable, the entertainment consisting in the gradual dissipation of this illusion, evidently requires the airiest and gayest of touches; but the climax, when the hero, his taste for independence recovered, begins to live again and succeeds at one stroke in getting rid of the pug and avoiding a second marriage, is reached by a process of leaden prolixity, with every point hammered out in a frenzy of emphasis. This exaggerated emphasis seems, in fact, the only native thing that these Italian writers have about them; take away their special *bravura*, the dreadful flourish of their rich, rank, pseudo-Ciceronian manner, and nothing remains but a little kernel of second-rate Parisian product. The very language has lost all raciness of idiomatic flavour. It would be interesting to inquire into the causes of this disease. Chief among them, no doubt, would have to be noted the extraordinary effectiveness of the forms of expression devised by the French genius, which, with their finality and logical clearness, have led most of the world captive; but a large part would also have to be assigned to the peculiar weaknesses of Italy—to her lack of any more than superficial unity, to the very richness and diversity of her dialects, and, in the last resort, to the uneasy self-consciousness which comes from a sense of political inferiority. Not only Italian fiction, but poetry too is touched with this deadly plagiarism of the spirit, of which it would be possible to discover the seeds even in the rugged Carducci, although he and his gentler successor at Bologna, Pascoli, to whom, along with Carducci, Professor Mignon devotes some well-informed pages in his *Études de Littérature Italienne* (Paris, Hachette, 3 fr. 50), seem to belong to a nobler race than the writers of to-day who, while struggling to assert their personality, remain, if they are anything, mere satellites of the coteries of Paris.

Consider Mr. Francesco Chiesa, one of whose objects is said to be the preservation of the Italian tongue in its struggle against competitors in the Canton Ticino. If this is true, his *Istorie e Favole* (A. F. Formiggini, Genoa) are a curious, even a tragic, comment on my remarks ; for here we have a writer active on one side of a struggle between nationalities, yet drawing all his inspiration from the foreigner. Mr. Chiesa's stories are a hash of Renaissance fantasies, a hodge-podge of pagan myth, of catholicism and of romance, such as has often been served up done to a turn by Anatole France and seems scarcely worth doing again. Here the French influence is palpable, and receives no disguise from a style which is often praised as sober and incisive. But allowance must be made for Italian exaggeration ; if there is sobriety, it is the sobriety of complete dulness.

The simplicity of Mr. Chiesa's case is not typical, however. The disease of spiritual plagiarism usually runs into subtler shapes, which, though they are infinite, seem in Italy to have one common characteristic, an exuberance of convulsive agitation. This agitation is like that of a man in a fever of self-distrust, who knows that there is something wrong with him and cannot quite make out what ; he casts about frantically for some attitude which will bring him salvation, but the quest is always vain, because salvation cannot come by attitudes. It is sometimes as exaggerated hatred of the past, and sometimes as exaggerated love of the past, that this self-distrust appears. The former, as embodied in the Futurists, has won notoriety abroad, and is strong in Mr. Giovanni Papini's *Un uomo finito* (Florence, Libreria della Voce) ; the latter in a very different book, Mr. Antonio Beltramelli's *Le Novelle della Guerra* (Milan, Fratelli Treves). Both spring from the same bitter root, that mood of exasperation and disillusionment which harps on the degradation of an Italy treated as an old curiosity shop, a villeggiatura for the idle rich of Europe, a street-walker among the nations, and which so strangely strikes the foreigner who admires the progress which she has made since 1870 and her great achievements in the sciences. There is indeed something strained and artificial about all the literatures of patriotic revival so fashionable just now ; not even the resources of M. Maurice Barrés' exquisite art can quite reconcile us to his glorification of the parish pump. That nations are to be saved by splitting into their component parts, each part a focus of the ancestral virtues that cling to the soil, is not very plausible at the best; and when the ideas of M. Barrés have been passed through the romantic Italian mind, and emerge exhausted of their content and unadorned by any accomplishment of style, the result is not attractive. Both Mr. Papini and Mr. Beltramelli are furiously *paesani*, the one of the grey-green Tuscan landscape, the other of the broad quiet spaces of the Romagna. Mr. Beltramelli is bellicose as well; he is a voice of that section of feeling, at present dominant, for which the return to ancestral virtue means a policy of military conquest. Imagine Mr. Kipling's imperial enthusiasm and ferocity against black men multiplied tenfold, with all the admirable realism left out and the Latin ideal of glory substituted for the English ideal of the strong silent public-school boy, and you have some idea of Mr. Beltramelli's sketches of the Tripolitan campaign, which he hails as the beginning, after an era of lethargy, of a new *risorgimento*. It is symptomatic that even the introduction to a new edition of the collection of Dalmatian popular ballads which Niccolo Tommaseo published in 1841 (*Canti Illirici*, Milan, Libreria editrice Milanese, 1912) cannot refrain from dragging in the Libyan war as the resumption by Italy of " her interrupted renovation."

The fact is, megalomania is a stock result of neurotic self-consciousness. In the struggle to assert his personality the patient jealously watches the actions of others in order to outdo them, and he has his eye on others even in his abysses of despair. Thus at every point on the scale he is incurably imitative; he is unable, as the phrase is, to " be himself." Mr. Papini's *Un uomo finito* is a complete anatomy of this morbid state, and therefore, though devoid of artistic merit, is a fascinating book. In language which is meant to be vigorous, but is merely turgid, he gives us, in the first person, the self-revelation of a man who is played out. The hero begins by hating society; he ransacks all departments of philosophy, scholarship and culture, he burns with literary ambition, he founds a review ; then, ever unsatisfied, he dreams of omnipotence ; he will impose his will on the world, he will be God. Failing in this enterprise, he sinks into decay ; but in the end he revives and declares that he still has unpleasant surprises in store for his enemies. " I still have something to say, and time before me ; in my house there is always white paper in abundance." May he live to cover many reams of this paper without misgivings ! His book is a compendium of all the qualities characteristic of Italian literature to-day—absence of sense of humour, insincerity, inability to observe life at first-hand, tasteless extravagance, and that submission to the influence of foreign culture which is none the less abject because combined with an angry desire to shake off the yoke. " Is it not possible," he cries at one moment in the false frankness of his confessions, " a thousand times possible that I am nothing but a frigid reader of books, always being warmed up at the fire of others, that I have mistaken the submissive grumbling of an ambitious soul for the bubbling of a vein that is quick to overflow and to gush, to refresh the thirsty earth and to mirror the sky ? " It is more than possible ; it is certain.

THE GALLERIES

By O. RAYMOND DREY

Gino Severini

GINO SEVERINI paints what he feels, what he chooses to feel, what he is naturally disposed to feel, if you will, with an amazing virtuosity. The studies in movement shown at the Marlborough Gallery in Duke Street for two or three weeks in April and May were full of technical resource, of lively draughtsmanship, of an almost baffling inventiveness. Relatively simple drawings of dancers, highly complex works in which colour, line and tone span heterodoxically into whirling compositions—with scarcely an exception they were effective as a pistol shot. What is even more, they were pleasantly effective. The line was strong and sweeping, instinct with movement : the colour, where colour was used, made cunning play with its whites and lemons and bright greens against a heavier puce.

I write so far without reference to Severini's æsthetic, without any thought of his theories or the ultimate value of his work ; without any valuing of " dynamism " as an emotional stimulant. Rather pathetically, Severini himself said a good deal about his theories and beliefs in an introduction to the catalogue, and in notes about the pictures. I am not going to argue with him. I have a natural respect for terms, and the painter in his headlong innocence is a disarming opponent.

Indeed, I am concerned far less with his theories, whether technical or æsthetic, than with the quality of his perceptions. His theories, as I understand them, I grant him with enthusiasm. A working theory is always chock-full of interest, in painting just as much as in bootmaking. I don't mind at all being " placed in the centre of the picture " (Technical Manifesto of Futurist Painting). It is quite a reasonable thing for a painter to try to do ; it is not by any means merely a frivolous thing to say that the middle of a picture is as proper a place as any for the critic. Every one who has tried to express movement statically, and nearly all painters and sculptors have tried consciously to do that, has been set theory-making in the attempt. It would be as foolish to blame Severini for theorising as it would be to blame Michaelangelo or Leonardo da Vinci or Dürer or Cézanne. It is impossible to do any sort of work without theory.

But the quality of his perceptions—that is a different thing altogether. The perceptions of a painter are his power of giving; that is to say of creation. There are obviously degrees of perception, which we call higher or lower according to our personal predilections. And here, because we are really at grips, and because he is making a statement of faith, I must quote from Severini's introduction. After speaking of " the intensity and rapidity with which life is lived to-day," he says :

" We choose to concentrate our attention on things in motion because our modern sensibility is particularly qualified to grasp the idea of speed. Heavy, powerful motor-cars rushing through the crowded streets of our great cities, dancers reflected in the fairy ambience of light and colour, aeroplanes flying above the heads of an excited throng. . . . These sources of emotion satisfy our sense of the lyric and dramatic universe, better than do two pears and an apple."

Now this attitude towards life may imply strength or violence ; it is a matter of opinion. To my mind Severini's perceptions are hectic rather than profound and imaginative. It is not a question of realism. All art, in so far as it is the expression of personal emotion, of personal vision, is realistic. To the dreamer dreams are reality. But to be impressed by a realisation of the complexities of modern life is an admission of weakness, a negation of personality. To be driven by such a realisation to worship of the outward signs of these complexities is the last sign of abject self-surrender, of Juggernaut belief. For surely the real force behind Severini's delight in the movement of omnibuses and can-can dancers, behind all his dexterity in expressing the " dynamism " of swirling fêtes and tube railways, is not joy, but fear. And fear, it seems to me, is a bad master of the arts.

MUSIC

By W. DENIS BROWNE

Beethoven, Elgar, Debussy

MUSIC during May and June means a sea of recitals at the rate of about forty or fifty a week. No single individual could hope to cope with them even if he wished to. As a matter of fact they are all much of a muchness. The same things are done over and over again, particularly by the pianists. I am left wondering whether Beethoven wrote anything besides the Waldstein Sonata or Brahms anything except the Sonata in F minor. Occasionally a singer like Elena Gerhardt or Julia Hostater appears, and makes you feel that recitals are sometimes justified; or a pianist like Petri or Pachmann. But the general run of concerts, as I have said, is monotonous at this time of year.

The London Symphony Orchestra has given three concerts of varying interest, the best of them being the first. Mengelberg conducted a very vital performance of Beethoven's C Minor Symphony and made a great impression with "Also sprach Zarathustra." It is one of Strauss' directest and most musical works, and was played with a refreshing enthusiasm. When Strauss is forced to think in music he really can achieve something: it is when he tries to be funny ("Till Eulenspiegel" excepted) or satirical that he fails. The second concert showed Mengelberg as a tyrant rather than a conductor. Perhaps he was angry at having to play Mr. Haydn Wood's unfortunate concerto—which most of the critics seemed to judge by unnecessarily advanced standards. The composer knows his business, but he should not have allowed so early a work to be produced at a time like the present. It was probably good enough and clever enough when it was written, but he could surely do something better now. At least I hope for his own sake that he can; for though sincerely and averagely well constructed, the concerto was both sentimental and verbose.

At the last concert Nikisch conducted the Choral Symphony with the Leeds Chorus. Comparison is immediately suggested with two other recent performances. The first, under Safonov, was perfectly straightforward and simple, without originality but not disfigured by mannerisms. The chorus sang rather tamely and without much grip. The second under Sir Henry Wood, was astonishingly perfect, but too mannered. The conductor's sense of detail was as usual so strong that the main outlines of the music were lost sight of. The Birmingham chorus sang magnificently—too well, in fact. Their enormous, rather hard, volume of tone is quite disconcerting to one who expects a chorus to sound like human voices and not like an organ or an assembly of expressive trumpets ; technically, they seemed perfect.

When Nikisch and the Leeds chorus took their turn, the result was different again. Niskisch gets his effects by suavity rather than violence. He humours his orchestra, he does not bully them like Mengelberg. His *tempi* were all over the place, as generally happens when a conductor is striving for an " individual " rendering of anything—but Nikisch has such a strong sense of line that he was able to blend all his vagaries into a logical whole. One may not agree with his details—at any rate they always form part of a perfectly definite conception : if in this case the symphony sounded quite new, the line taken was perfectly clear and consistent—the emphasis was on the human and material side, not on the abstract. The Leeds chorus were not quite so hard and brilliant as the Birmingham chorus, and I was grateful to them because they did not spend all their time making " points." But they have not the same vigour and volume as the others. Nor has Nikisch the same blunt vigour as Mengelberg, though he has more brains than Wood. I should like to hear yet another performance of the Symphony, and I should cast it for Mengelberg, the London Symphony Orchestra and the Birmingham chorus. That would unite virtuosity and power with unequalled control. I am afraid though that we shall never hear the choral part sound anything else than simply inhuman, whereas Beethoven intended it to sound superhuman.

Sir Edward Elgar thoroughly succeeded in swamping the Leeds chorus with his orchestra in " The Music Makers." As for Miss Muriel Foster, she stood no chance whatever : she may have had more to do than to open and shut her mouth at stated intervals, but there was no means of judging. She was only audible twice. If Elgar were not by this time beyond hope as a composer, " The Music Makers " would make one despair : as things are it must be accepted as a normal product of a talent very much on the down-grade.

Debussy has been prominent lately, and it is extraordinarily pleasant to be able to listen to him with the strain of unfamiliarity removed. Mr. Walter Morse Rummel has been playing the second book of Preludes. Covent Garden has given " Pelléas et Mélisande," and Mr. Beecham has produced the orchestral suite " Printemps." Mr. Rummel's sensitive playing of the Preludes made them sound wonderfully clear simply because he suppressed all the irrelevant details. On paper there bristle cascades of notes. With Mr. Rummel they were over and gone almost before they could be realised—an almost inaudible catch of the breath, no more. On the whole the Preludes are unequal. Five are good—" Feuilles mortes," " La Puerta del Vino," " Bruyères," " General Lavine," " Canope." From the point of view of rhythm and colour, " La Puerta del Vino " is the best thing Debussy has done since " La Soirée dans Grenade " (also a *habanera*). On the other hand, he has written nothing before so pointless as " Hommage à S. Pickwick, Esq., P.P.M.P.C." It is neither a good joke nor good music. The rest of the preludes are inclined either to calculated vagueness or to extreme virtuosity. With the exception of two they might all exchange names without anyone being the wiser. The whole of the second book leaves Debussy just a little higher and drier than the first book. That contained nothing so stupid as " Hommage à S. Pickwick, Esq." This has nothing in it that reaches the level of " La Cathédrale Engloutie."

" Pelléas et Mélisande," having once again struggled as far

as production, was very beautifully performed at Covent Garden. The orchestra never becomes part of the opera until the third act, but the orchestration is bound up with the poem all the time. The actual music itself is so tenuous as to be often negligible, but its colour and the instrumental grouping—in which no instrument is ever used to reinforce, but only for purposes of contrast—are so intimately connected with the remoteness of the persons on the stage that there is a complete fusion between the music and the drama of a kind that Wagner never dreamed of.

There is little to be said for " Printemps." It is unusual for Debussy to be vulgar or commonplace, but here he is both. What used to be charming in the " Petite Suite " is combined with the heavy sense of humour that nowadays makes him think a sham cake-walk the funniest thing in the world. The orchestra were not any more enthusiastic over the Debussy than over Rimsky-Korsakov's " Antar," which they ambled through in a rather dull way. It is arid stuff at best, over-descriptive and yet not realistic enough : about as good as the older type of average Greek play music at the Universities. Mr. Beecham's programmes are so interesting on paper : it is a pity that they sometimes disappoint in performance. Still he is the only conductor who takes a real interest in modern music. Incidentally he has produced a *coloratura* singer in Miss Florence Macbeth, who has a future before her.

For Product Safety Concerns and Information please contact our EU representative GPSR@taylorandfrancis.com
Taylor & Francis Verlag GmbH, Kaufingerstraße 24, 80331 München, Germany

www.ingramcontent.com/pod-product-compliance
Lightning Source LLC
Chambersburg PA
CBHW081356090726
47908CB00011B/2690

* 9 7 8 0 3 6 7 1 8 0 1 0 2 *